Borderline Personality Disorder

The Ultimate Self Help Guide to Developing the Right Understanding of BPD + Bonus: The Most Effective Treatment Method to Managing Emotions and Improving Relationships

Emerson Hooper

assurance.

The trademarks that are used are without any consent, and the publication of the trademark is without permission or backing by the trademark owner. All trademarks and brands within this book are for clarifying purposes only and are owned by the owners themselves, not affiliated with this document.

Contents

Introduction

This book offers to provide detailed and accurate information on Borderline Personality Disorder. It can help you offer advice and help you by expanding your understanding of Bipolar Personality Disorders. Borderline Personality Disorder has been shown to produce severe deficits in a wide variety of settings. When compared to other groups, patients with Borderline Personality Disorder (commonly known as BPD) have much higher rates of morbidity and death. Despite the fact that Borderline Personality Disorder has been studied more extensively than just about any personality disorder, it is still not fully understood. By reviewing in-depth published studies, this book provides a concise review of the most recent research on the comorbidity, prevalence, etiology, and treatment options of borderline personality disorder. Pervasive emotional instability, self-image problems, impulsivity, significant suicide ideation, and unstable interpersonal interactions are the fundamental characteristics of psychopathology that underlie Borderline Personality Disorder, which is a chronic psychiatric disease. The objective of this BPD book is to offer a more unified approach for the management and recognition of Borderline Personality Disorder.

Borderline Personality Disorder is significantly under-recognized, and treatment faces challenges. It is the most misunderstood and stigmatized mental health diagnosis. Carefully study each section, and good luck!

Chapter 1: What is Borderline Personality Disorder?

Borderline Personality Disorder is significantly under-recognized, and treatment faces challenges. It is the most misunderstood and stigmatized mental health diagnosis. Though people with BPD may struggle significantly with their symptoms, they're also some of the most sensitive, caring, and engaged clients.

It is a very serious diagnosis and requires the help of a licensed professional in order to really make the gains and get past some of the behavioral and emotional problems that people struggle with; it's not something to be taken lightly; in fact, there's a much higher rate of suicidal threats as well as suicidal behaviors and individuals who struggle with this.

1. Sense of Self

   People diagnosed with BPD struggle with an unstable sense of who they are like people and are unable to trust themselves as well as others. So their views of themselves, as well as others, shift constantly from positive to negative. Shifting extremes, for example, one minute your friends are the best people in the world, and the next, by the smallest misunderstanding, they're the words people you've ever met. This can happen with family, friends, spouses, and basically any other relationship.

2. Emotional States

Their emotional states switch quickly and frequently, which is very disturbing for them, and they often go to extreme lengths to numb out their emotions or overcompensate for what their feeling. For example, they can go from feeling euphoric to depress in a minute. Often, it is challenging to keep track of what triggers this change in emotion.

3. Impulsive Behavior

Because of the frequent change in emotional states, they struggle with modulating and managing their emotions. Normally they will try distracting themselves from numbing out the pain and stress. Commonly this behavior involves self-harm, excessive drugs, excessive alcohol, risky sexual behavior, and hanging relationships frequently.

4. Unpredictable Emotions

A noticeable tendency to shift between the state of extreme emotional dysregulation (so going from happy to sad really quickly, as mentioned before) to a state of feeling empty and numb or detached and this is difficult to handle for both the patient as well as the people around him/her.

1.1: History

Within U. S., Adolph Stern created the phrase "borderline personality disorder" in 1938. (Most of the personality disorders were introduced first in Europe). According to Adolph Stern, a patient population that fits neither into the psychoneurotic category nor into the psychotic category was found, and he coined the term "borderline" to describe what he perceived as a condition that "bordered" on other diseases.

To characterize a consistent pattern of behavior and functioning defined by dysfunction and suggesting disturbed self-organization, Otto Kernberg developed the phrase "borderline personality organization"; it has since become widely used. The symptoms and behavior associated with borderline personality, regardless of the underlying psychological structures, could become more widely recognized, including an extremely insecure self-image, fears of abandonment, rapid mood swings, denial, and a high proclivity toward suicidal ideation, as mentioned previously. Psychotic risk factors such as delusions and hallucinations can sometimes occur on a temporary basis in patients. The features that are today recognized as a borderline personality disorder (BPD) first were stated by Gunderson and Kolb in 1978, and they have subsequently been included in current psychiatric classification systems.

In addition to anxiety, eating depression, and eating disorders such as post-traumatic stress disorder (PTSD), bulimia, drug addiction disorders, and mood dysfunctions, a borderline personality disorder is frequently diagnosed as co-morbid with other mental illnesses such as bipolar disorder. Its placement on the 'borderline' of additional diseases, or as a result of conceptual ambiguity, has resulted in its being classified as such (with which it is commonly clinically misunderstood). There might be a massive overlap between psychotic disorders and other conditions. In serious cases, patients may experience both visual and auditory hallucinations, as well as powerful delusional thoughts, but these are typically brief and correlated with times of intense emotional disorder and can be distinguished from the fundamental clinical symptoms of schizophrenia and other related disorders, such as bipolar disorder.

Due to the high levels of co-morbidity, it is uncommon to come across someone who has a sheer case of BPD. Several people assume that borderline personality disorder would never be classified as a personality disorder since it intersects with other disorders. However, this is not always true. A bipolar disorder or a disorder of self must be used to categorize the condition instead. Some have proposed that borderline personality disorder BPD could be regarded as a kind of prolonged post-traumatic stress disorder (PTSD) because of its relationship to prior trauma and evident similarities to post-traumatic stress disorder (PTSD). A borderline personality disorder is significantly more regular than the other forms of personality disorders, and it is perhaps the most researched of the personality disorders amidst these misgivings. However, while some persons with borderline personality disorder emerge from caring and happy homes, turbulence and lack of relationships are more likely to foster borderline personality development and to be the focus of preventative measures in these patients.

It is important to recognize borderline personality disorder from the apparent "borderline intelligence," which is a completely separate and unique notion from a borderline personality disorder. Individuals with significant learning impairments, on the other hand, are more likely than the general population to exhibit borderline personality characteristics (especially self-harm). Borderline personality disorder can manifest itself in a variety of ways. The majority of persons suffer mental health problems in their adolescent years, although they may not seek treatment from mental health professionals until later. Based on those who have received therapy or an official medical examination, fifty percent of persons recover to the extent where they can't fit the criteria for borderline personality disorder five to ten years after being diagnosed with the illness. It's uncertain how much of this is attributable to therapy; research suggests that a substantial amount of recovery is spontaneous and is accompanied by more personality and awareness on the part of the patient.

The stage at which borderline personality disorder can present itself is a point of contention in the scientific community. Due to the fact that their identities are still growing, many individuals feel it cannot or should not be detected in people under the age of eighteen. Despite the fact that the classification is likely to be found in the Diagnostics and Statistical Manual of Mental Disorders, the fourth edition [DSM-IV; American Psychological Association, 1994] is based on the rules as adults with additional cautions). However, borderline symptoms and characteristics can often be seen at a much relatively young age, perhaps as early as adolescence. Its first manifestations in teenage groups are now garnering more awareness than they did previously.

A borderline personality disorder is associated with considerable impairment, especially when it comes to sustaining successful relations. This is because of the intimate and psychological dysfunction that it causes. It has been observed that the degree of borderline personality disorder behaviors and symptoms is related to the severity of family, vocational, and social limitations in a small number of individuals. Nevertheless, this isn't always the case, and particular persons with borderline personality disorder who also prefer to be borderline in other aspects of their lives may be capable of performing at exceptionally high rates in their respective fields. Individuals suffering from borderline personality disorder hurt themself on a frequent basis, generally in an attempt to relieve excruciating pain. This results in significant bodily damage and impairment for many of these individuals. Moreover, suicide is still a common occurrence in people who have a borderline personality disorder and can occur years after the first signs and symptoms show.

It is important to note that while the diagnosis for borderline personality disorder is generally favorable, with the proportion of persons inability to achieve the diagnostic criteria after five years, it is important to remember that a small proportion of humans experience reoccurring symptoms until later in life. Sometimes, recurrent self-harm in the aged can be a source of worry, and the possibility that this is linked to borderline personality disorder must be considered. Nonetheless, the sickness is substantially less prevalent in older than it does in the youth, and, in contrast to other mental illnesses, healing from the illness is significantly least likely to be followed by a recurrence than it is in the other age groups.

1.2: Types of BPD

There are a number of forms of borderline personality disorder. As per Theodore Millon, a specialist in behavioral disorders, there are 4 distinct kinds of BPD:

1. BPD which is discouraged

2. Petulant BPD

3. Impulsive behavior BPD

4. Self-destructive behavior BPD

1. Borderline personality disorder that has been discouraged

Despite being depressed, the discouraged borderline exhibits submissive and clinging behavior and is able to see outside of a group situation. They are generally overflowing with despair and fury, directed towards individuals in their immediate environment, under the face of things. Borderline individuals who are sad are more likely to engage in self-mutilation or possibly attempt suicide. They desire to be loved, yet they also avoid others, believe they are unworthy and are vulnerable to depressive disorders.

BPD can be classified into four subgroups. A few of these types are BPD that has been discouraged. When a person has discouraged borderline personality disorder, the reliant parts of their personality disorder determine a great deal of how they will be expected to behave and act. According to Psychology Today, an individual with a discouraged borderline personality disorder might look to others as if they have a committed personality disorder on the surface. This personality exhibits signs of codependence in the majority of their relationships.

In many cases, the reliance of a rejected borderline type is most evident when they rely on somebody for whom dependence is inappropriate, such as an associate or a possible love interest, among other people. When this type is associated with one or more of the other borderline disorder categories, a person with this type may look serious or gloomy to everyone else. The disheartened borderline is characterized by neediness and a submissive "disciple" attitude toward others. From the outside, though, this person may look hesitant or, in the worst-case scenario, timid. In most cases, they are tortured inwardly by their lack of accountability as well as hostility directed at people in their immediate vicinity. Individuals suffering from this form of borderline disorder may resort to self-harming behaviors such as self-harm or suicide.

Who is suffering from this disorder?

Bipolar disorder (BPD) and its disabling BPD subtype can afflict both males and females of all ages or backgrounds; however, the disease is much more frequent in females than in males. It could be related to a biological factor such as low estrogen levels, or it could be related to a bias generated by institutionalized discrimination against women. Women, based on specific research, are more likely than males to seek therapy, be recommended to seek treatment or be officially mistaken or diagnosed with borderline personality disorder, while men are less likely. This decision is established most frequently throughout adolescence, and it is usually made even before the ending of the teenage years or the start of early maturity. It is anticipated that around 1.6 percent of all Americans will suffer from BPD in any given year.

Indications of BPD Disillusionment

As per the DSM-V, the bipolar disorder manifests itself through a variety of indications and symptoms. When seeking to identify borderline personality disorder (BPD) or the dissatisfied borderline subtype, doctor search for the symptoms listed below. These are afflictions of the personality's ability to operate:

- Disabilities in the ability to serve oneself. Examples of these types of impairments include having a disordered or poor self-image, being extremely critical of oneself, having continuous feelings of emptiness, and experiencing tension-induced dissociative experiences. It is possible that this is caused by inconsistency in one's priorities, career goals, values, or aspirations in nature.

- Deterioration of interpersonal skills. Enhanced and intense identifying of alleged criticism or reluctance, as well as black-and-white thinking about individuals – most people are known as either bad or good illustrations of these types of impairments. Reduced compassion, which can be manifested as a smaller power to consider others' perspectives. When there is a difficulty with cognitive function, it is possible that there will be an issue with affection. These difficulties can emerge as very strong and problematic relationships that are characterized by high tension, mistrust, a fear of abandonment, neediness, and retreat at various points throughout the relationship.

- There are several other characteristics that distinguish a person with borderline BPD from the general public. Some of the indications and symptoms that may be present are as follows:

- Without a doubt, stimulated emotions

- Emotional skills that are in flux

- Mood swings

- Anxiety over losing one's composure

- Anxiety, tension, concern, uneasiness, or fear symptoms that are more severe.

- Fixation on poor practices from the past or on the likelihood of future bad behaviors

- Feelings that appear to be excessive or strong in relation to the reason for their occurrence

- Confusion and dissatisfaction

- Uncertainty and a lack of self-consciousness

- Dangerous risk-taking behaviors that are not concerned with the repercussions

- Rudeness, particularly when there is a sense of rejection or judgment

- Increased dependency and loss of independence, as well as concern over an "unavoidable" sense of autonomy

- Anxiety over being rejected

- Anxiety associated with loss

- Feelings of powerlessness or depression

- Humiliation

- Problems are adhering to or devising plans of action.

- Suicidal actions or ideas are present.

- Impulsivity

- Determination brought forth by distress

- Dissociation, or "zoning out," as well as trouble concentrating

- BPD symptoms that are specific to the discouraged borderline include the following.

- even while demanding a critical role; passive and subservient

- Loyalty, but only to an extreme extent.

- There has been a threat to the constant stream of thoughts.

- Feelings of self-victimization and self-persecution; believing that others are always ill-intentioned or assaulting

- Excessive reliance on others for survival

- Self-deprivation (as a kind of resistance to self-indulgence) is deeply based on feelings of unworthiness.

- There are some heartbreaking scenes.

- Substance addiction is a problem.

- Due to a lack of self-confidence, fragility, and insecurity, he is humble.

- Reliance on imagination as a means of escaping, as demonstrated by involvement in fictional entertainment (novels, comics, movies, etc.)

- Having constant thoughts of inadequacy and vulnerability.

- Deliberate loss or annihilation of things, whether via physical aggression against one's goods or through a cycle of acquiring, selling, and giving away one's assets

- Capable of being persuaded by others, yet when acting in accordance with one's own interests, it is called for.

- Criticisms of recurrent or chronic disease, which might include somatic complaints

- Having a sense of hopelessness, powerlessness, helplessness, and depression

- Suffering from feelings of emptiness

Relationships between causes and effects

As is true for all mental health problems, pinpointing the specific cause of BPD or its discouraged type is difficult, and this is especially true for BPD. As per experts, the etiology of this illness is complicated and not readily or quickly identifiable at first glance. While borderline personality disorder (BPD) is complex and complicated, involving a wide range of different life events, most specialists in the area appear to agree on particular probable contributing factors. Below are some of the factors that contribute to and are related to:

- The presence of congenital brain abnormalities, such as a smaller than normal amygdala.

- The study of genetics, particularly in DAT and the genes

DRD4 and chromosome nine

- Bipolar disorder (BPD) may be linked with post-traumatic stress disorder (PTSD).

- Community and personal stability levels, as well as other environmental concerns (away from trauma)

- Social variables are affecting social practices when a kid is involved.

- Childhood abuse, including abuse and neglect, which may include sexual abuse in some cases

- There are also neurobiological factors, such as estrogen concentrations.

- Diagnosis is difficult because of the complexities involved.

Even the most skilled mental health professional may have difficulty diagnosing borderline personality disorder and its subtypes. Per a 2011 Scientific American report, the afflictions assessment is frequently incorrect in some manner or another. Women who suffer from the condition are more likely than males to have co-occurring disorders, which makes an accurate diagnosis more difficult. Clinical depression, anorexia, anxiety, antisocial personality disorder, and addiction are some of the additional illnesses that are frequently considered co-morbid with BPD, according to the American Psychological Association. A low sense of self-worth or a negative self-image are common characteristics of many of these co-occurring illnesses.

Discouragement and Its Treatment

Patients who want to live a useful and luxurious lifestyle to the greatest of their ability must be evaluated and addressed for bipolar disorder. It is particularly important since bipolar disorder is linked with a significant risk of suicide in the general population. The tendency to self-harm and suicidal ideation among people with bipolar disorder accounts for a substantial proportion of suicides each year; thus, any self-harm or violent ideation on the part of someone with bipolar disorder should be addressed immediately and treated extremely seriously. As soon as you or anybody with whom you associate is at risk of committing suicide, get help as soon as possible.

Currently, psychotherapy is the most appropriate method for dealing with and treating BPD. Although there is no one-size-fits-all medicine to treat bipolar disorder, several of the co-morbid conditions that frequently accompany bipolar disorder may be addressed with prescription medication, which boosts the therapy rate of success of the condition. It's crucial to note that, while these medications will not cure bipolar disorder, they can pave the way for more successful treatment of the disorder through psychotherapy.

The most common co-morbid diseases are depression and anxiety, both of which are treated with medication while the patient undergoes psychotherapy for generalized borderline personality disorder (BPD). In addition to treating psychotic and paranoid symptoms, antipsychotics can also be used to address depression, anxiety, impulsivity, suicidal inclinations, and rage. When dealing with a patient who has bipolar disorder, it is critical to search for co-morbid signs and treats them as necessary. Co-morbid conditions must be addressed prior to care being initiated, and therapy must be initiated. In the case of borderline personality disorder (BPD), for example, substance misuse should be removed as a contributing cause to problematic behavior before genuine treatment can begin. If this is not the case, the client's cognitive capacity may be impaired, making it hard for a professional to conduct a complete evaluation on them.

2. Petulant BPD

Unpredictability, anger, aggressiveness, and impatience are all characteristics of the petulant personality type. They are stubborn, pessimistic, and bitter most of the time. You experience tremendous feelings of worthlessness and wrath, which you alternate between. This propensity for erupting is a result of these fury-fueled eruptions of rage. Petulant borderlines are terrified of being let down by somebody, but they can't seem to avoid the urge to rely on anyone in order to feel secure. They are hostile in a passive-aggressive manner and may indulge in self-harming activities in order to seek attention.

What does it look like?

For example, A couple tried counseling at the Optimum Performance Center when they were 20 years old for the petulant borderline personality disorder that had made maintaining a stable marriage nearly difficult for years.

Nobody could deny that they were raised in a rigorous environment. Their dad was an alcoholic, and he never met or spoken to her mother before. They were pulled from their house while he was six years old, along with their mother and brother.

They were reared after their mother's parental rights were removed, and they were put in three separate foster homes during their childhood. Their adoptive "parents" were wonderful; they encouraged them in their schoolwork and included her in all of the family's activities. They grew accustomed to them, but he never developed a deep emotional attachment to them. They considered it a primary focus to hide this information from their family members' ears. It didn't matter if the information was big or tiny; it didn't make a difference to anyone. They took pleasure in the knowledge that they were not dependent on them and that they were completely ignorant of everything there was to discover about him.

They liked their mom, but they didn't care for them at all. A similar statement may be made about his peers, particularly as he got older. A minor setback for others, such as a buddy becoming ill and having to cancel plans, became an excruciating ordeal for Kyle, who turned to self-harm to relieve her misery and "inform" people that he was not okay. Kyle's story is one of hope and determination. If their new acquaintances did not meet his high expectations, they would be disappointed or furious, informing them that "if you loved me..." they would do whatever it took to make them seem beautiful. Their partners were typically incapable of withstanding it, and they only had a few partnerships that persisted longer than a year.

What are the indications and symptoms of petulant borderline personality disorder?

A number of severe borderline personality disorder symptoms were seen in them, including the following:

- A reluctance to express one's opinions.

- Fierce outbreaks of rage

- feelings of unworthiness, un-lovability, and unacceptability

- Feeling anxious in social circumstances

- The fear of being forsaken by one's family.

- A desire to exert influence over people

- Are you unsatisfied with your current or past relationships?

- Recurring disorders include alcoholism and eating disorders, to name a few instances.

- In relationships, mistrust of others/paranoia is common.

- Suicidal inclinations are present.

- Dramatic shifts in one's emotional state

- Giving ultimatums in marriages is a bad idea.

- "Demonstrating" to her that someone does not care about her.

- Constantly on the lookout for proof

- There is a good thing about interplay in collaborative relationships.

- wishing for others to feel awful about themselves for their actions (or lack thereof)

- Isolating oneself from the rest of society.

- Suicidal or self-injurious behaviors were used to exercise influence over others in this situation.

- At the heart of some petulant BPD, behaviors are feelings of abandonment, self-worth, and a reluctance to self-soothe, among other things. By utilizing the right treatment, you will be capable of overcoming petulant borderline personality disorder.

The only method to cope with a BPD diagnosis that refuses to cooperate

Commonly, youngsters were admitted to two outpatient treatment clinics for the symptoms of BPD. Nonetheless, they received only a limited respite. When you were present, they learned about mental health issues and how to detect their symptoms, but they did not fully get how their illnesses may influence their long-term aspirations until you explained it to them. Their incentive to participate in the rehabilitation process from BPD was very lacking.

Due to their prior suicide attempt at their college home when they were 20 years old, they were requested to leave college in order to receive therapy. They chose the Optimum Performance Institute or OPI since our focus on aiding young individuals with borderline personality disorder (BPD) with their rehabilitation and transition to adulthood looked to be a better match for their requirements.

Their psychiatrist, who joined the OPI team shortly after they did, worked closely with them to untangle their BPD pattern, and develop a treatment plan that was more appropriate for their complicated symptoms and challenges.

In the beginning, they worked on acquiring the techniques of dialectical behavior therapy (DBT) to the point where they were second nature. Self-soothing exercises were the main focus of their training as they learned how to manage their emotions when they were out of hand.

They and their doctor decided that they were in a position to go deep into their memories and probe into their experiences. They had not been prepared to deal with a situation that had occurred when they were in recovery as children until they and their counselor thought they had had sufficient experience with dialectical behavior modification techniques in real-life situations.

Having to uncover those scars and explore the sentiments and convictions that were hidden behind them was excruciatingly difficult for me. OPI colleagues who've been through the recovery process themselves encouraged her that she would make it and shared their most forceful coping strategies. They took visits to the seaside and engaged in a hip-hop session for a few hours each week to get their minds off of the intense therapeutic practice they were through.

It didn't take long for them to realize that they got to bring their newly acquired abilities — particularly their interpersonal skills — to the trial outside of the OPI atmosphere. They were offered a position at a vet clinic since they hoped to one day work as a veterinarian. They gathered with the executive director till the start of the new school year to plan out the courses they would need to take in order to be accepted into veterinarian school. A few classes were taken at a neighboring community college, and they talked with their OPI personal trainer to determine which research approaches would be most beneficial to them.

With the assistance of the OPI team, they worked and studied for eight months, juggling education, careers, engagements, and therapy in the process. When they returned home, they were prepared since they knew exactly what caused their BPD signs and how to cope with them when they resurfaced in the future. They came home with a number of stable connections forged at work, in college, and at OPI, so they were anxious to build on her success at OPI by repeating her accomplishment. When petulant BPD must be handled on your own, it is quite unusual.

Was that the only method to obtain therapy for BPD that is petty in nature?

The symptoms of petulant BPD are generally difficult to handle on your own. It is normal for the growth in borderline personality disorder to be accompanied by great discomfort, which is compounded by BPD symptoms that can sometimes lead to the very creature you are avoiding: dysfunctional interpersonal interactions.

3. Impulsive BPD.

It is typical to have a charming, lively, and appealing spontaneous borderline personality. In search of pleasures and fast-growing boredom, you may be superficial, flirty, and evasive in your approach. Borderline impulsive individuals rely on notoriety and excitement to get them out of difficulty, and they frequently get themself into difficulties when they act first and think afterward. When people seek approval from those around them in order to avoid feeling rejected and abandoned, this can take the lead to material abuse and self-injurious act.

Impulsive bipolar disorder (IBD) is one of the four subtypes of bipolar disorder. It's highly effective among the four BPD groups and is the most common. It's quite familiar with borderline personality disorder, as per psychologist Theodore Million, who studies impulsive subtypes.

Signs or Symptoms of Impulsive Borderline Personality Disorder

When it comes to impetuous borderline personality disorder, the preceding indications and symptoms are frequently observed in those who have this subtype:

- Being flirtatious with someone, even if they aren't aware of it

- Intriguing, with an instinctual attraction to work with

- enigmatic and erratic

- Self-indulgence, comfortably making people laugh on a base level while disregarding deeper life experience or connections

- Increased capacity and favoritism toward laziness

- Chasing excitement and taking chances without regard for the consequences

- Efforts to gain attestation from others

- Disease symptoms that are chronic or recurring

In some cases, the common symptoms of the impulsive type are the same as or coincide with that of the more typical signs and symptoms of borderline personality disorder.

Generalized Borderline Disorder Signs and Symptoms

The following are among the symptoms and signals to be on alert for:

- Having a very low or unsteady sense of one's own value and identity

- Excessive self-criticism

- Persistent feelings of emptiness

- Experiencing psychotic states, especially when distressed

- Uncertainty about one's own best interest, aspirations, career direction, or basic principles

- Being oversensitive, particularly to perception, rejection, or criticism

- A tendency to idealize or despise those around

- Discontent and uncertainty about the unexpected

- Worry about losing control

- Broad and deep feelings of guilt

- Fear of becoming separated

- A sense of hopelessness and powerlessness

- A depressed mood

- Suicide attempts

- Difficulty devising or sticking to a plan

- Taking more risks, such as infidelity in marriage and betting

- Intolerance

The Impulsive Subclass of BPD and the Factors That Contribute to It

In the realm of mental disorders, it is difficult to determine the specific cause of a problem. Psychiatric illnesses are complex, and much of the research required to understand their origins are still in progress today.

Prevailing thoughts on mental illnesses are that they are the result of a variety of factors, neither of which are confirmed to have a bigger impact than others. Developmental injuries, neurological problems, neurobiological abnormalities, biology, effects on the environment, socioeconomic variables, and psychosocial traits are all basics that provide to the development of this disorder.

There are also several types of research being conducted on borderline personality disorder and its impulsive type, as well as the causes and connections that exist between the two. We do acknowledge that the following factors are in play:

- **Adversity During Childhood**

Childhood trauma is a typical incidence in people with bipolar disorder. Survivors have reported that violence and abandonment were two of the major childhood traumas they experienced, with sex assault being among the most frequent. Studies have discovered a high prevalence of caretaker failures and adultery in the childhood experiences of persons suffering from BPD. Adolescents with borderline personality disorder (BPD) frequently complain that their caretakers dismissed the authenticity of their feelings as kids and refused to provide the necessary safety. It has been discovered that caretakers who are emotionally absent and untrustworthy are the most prevalent commonality among persons with a borderline personality disorder or the impulsive type.

- **Neurobiological Factors to Consider**

BPD has been related to high estrogen levels in the body. Female hormone levels can fluctuate over their menstrual cycle, which can be observed occasionally. The treatment of severe

PMS must be differentiated from that of bipolar disorder, and individuals that already have endometriosis must not be put on hormone-related medication.

- **Abnormalities of the Cerebral Cortex**

There have been a number of other brain abnormalities associated with BPD that have been documented. It has been discovered that the amygdala and hippocampus, for instance, have decreased in size. People with BPD have lower levels of the prefrontal cortex than persons who may not have the disease, which is another sign of the disorder. Cortisol production, which is controlled by the hypothalamic-pituitary-adrenal pathway, is generally increased in patients suffering from bipolar disorder (BPD). Having excessive cortisol production throughout childhood may be the result of stressful developmental events that cause cortisol production. It might be caused by a high amount of hormone levels that exist prior to the onset of the disorder, causing sufferers to view events as distressing.

- **Genetic factors are a field of biology that is concerned with the study of genes.**

Genetic diversity is the subject of the BPD causal analysis. It is estimated that BPD has a heredity ratio of around 65 percent. The results of a study done in the Netherlands found that genetic effects account for 42 percent of the diversity in BPD symptoms among patients and that chromosome 9 is associated with BPD symptoms. Another gene, DRD4, which has been related to disordered binding as well as DAT, which has been connected to inhibitory regulatory problems, are two others that are now being studied for their potential role in the growth of bipolar disorder (BPD).

- **Other Points to Consider**

Other factors that may contribute to the development of BPD are also being investigated by researchers. Certain factors, such as familial stability and societal stability, are being examined because they have the potential to assist avoid the beginning of this disease. They have the potential to have a role in the development of BPD.

Identifying and diagnosing BPD of the aggressive variety

Identifying and diagnosing BPD has, undoubtedly, been a difficult task for a long time. Since Adolf Stern initially coined the term "borderline personality disorder" in 1938, mental health professionals have attempted to define the treatment and therapy for persons who have BPD. A number of issues complicate the evaluation of BPD in a clinical setting, adding to the difficulty of this type of task.

Patients with bipolar disorder (BPD) have a high prevalence of combination. Several folks who endure borderline personality disorder also suffer from severe depression, depressive symptoms, drug abuse, antisocial personality disorder, and eating disorders, to mention a few conditions. The presence of these issues can make it difficult for others to recognize BPD from a distance, and some of them, such as drug abuse, can make it difficult for a person's personal cognitive capacity and rehabilitation to develop.

Managing Borderline Personality Disorder (BPD)

The medicine available may fundamentally alter how an individual process and handles their illness, despite the fact that the highs and lows of daily life might be tough to stomach at times.

Individuals suffering from a borderline personality disorder (BPD) must get therapy as soon as feasible. Delaying treatment can aggravate the condition, which, if left untreated, can become extremely debilitating over time and cause death. Furthermore, BPD is directly or indirectly responsible for a substantial number of suicides each and every year. Therefore, any self-harm, suicidal thoughts, or self-mutilation or acts on the part of a person suffering from BPD must be handled and taken seriously as soon as possible. No matter how you or anyone you know is in danger of suicide, it is critical that you get psychiatric assistance as quickly as possible.

Although managing, controlling, and recovery from BPD may appear to be challenging, it is not insurmountably difficult. In actuality, testing has shown that BPD can be healed from, and people who suffer from it may strive toward leading a completely stable and fulfilling life.

Psychotherapy is a system of treatment that is commonly employed. A large amount of research has been conducted on borderline personality disorder (BPD) make use of psychotherapy. Cognitive behavior therapy, transference-focused therapy (TFT), dialectical behavior therapy, mentalization-based therapy (MBT), schema-focused therapy (SFT), and general psychological management are all effective treatment techniques for borderline personality disorder. MBT and DBT were two of the most effective treatments available, but the key to a successful treatment is determining which method works best for each person.

Medications on prescription

While there is currently no medicine that may cure BPD, drugs are frequently used to assist symptoms in conjunction with BPD in order to enhance overall therapy. For example, when the primary symptoms of BPD are addressed without diverting the effect of the other issues, anxiety, stress, anger, and impulsivity should also be addressed with medication. Medical management of these coexisting diseases is not only advantageous but is also considered crucial in the treatment of borderline personality disorder. It is critical to understand that, while there is currently no recognized therapy for borderline personality disorder, there is medication available to help manage the symptoms more effectively. Simply said, it is a matter of preparing the ground for more effective and beneficial handling of the overlap difficulties.

It is not necessary to live with impetuous style BPD to be a permanent source of the difficulty. Persons' capability to manage the complexities of daily life is greatly enhanced by treatment, which may fundamentally alter how they process and handle their illness.

The Optimal Performance Center is a pioneer in the treatment of borderline personality disorder in children and adolescents. The OPI Intensive has been dubbed "Best of Diagnosis" by

Psychology Today for its effectiveness in the treatment of borderline personality disorder. When it comes to BPD patients, OPI Intensive caters to their specific requirements and those of the members in the recovery program while also preserving a solid social framework. An engagement period of 30 days and a really revolutionary phase of 30 days are both included in the curriculum. Consequently, young individuals are considerably more equipped to deal with their BPD and to live freely and joyfully in adulthood as a result of this treatment.

Chapter 2: Myths About BPD

2.1: Individuals under eighteen are not affected by borderline personality disorder

It is currently considered to be one of the greatest widely accepted BPD hypotheses and beliefs. The present Diagnostic and Statistical Guide of Mental Illnesses (DSM) or previous editions of the DSM do not restrict the diagnosis of borderline personality disorder (BPD) in persons under the age of 18. We cannot accept that a psychiatrist does not recognize BPD until a teenager is seventeen and that he or she does not declare it until the adolescent becomes eighteen the following day. The quicker you obtain a verdict, the quicker you will be able to begin treatment.

2.2: Borderline personality disorder (BPD) is an uncommon condition

BPD is a condition that affects many people. Schizophrenia is a mental illness that affects approximately 2 million people in the United States and is well-known to several individuals. Not only is borderline personality disorder more common than schizophrenia, but it is also more frequent than borderline personality disorder in some cases. As per projection from a large study performed in 2008, over 14 million people in the

United States suffer from a borderline personality disorder. About 11 percent of psychiatric outpatients, 20 percent of hospitalized patients, and 6 percent of individuals who see their main health care physician are affected by BPD.

2.3: Lazy parenting is responsible for 8.3 percent of BPD cases

Parents are frequently blamed for their children's difficulties. However, there is no evidence that bad parenting is a contributing factor to BPD. Every scenario is different, and parents may be worsening their child's natural vulnerability in some cases. Regardless, the vast margin of parents are caring, authorized personnel who are unclear of how to best support their children. It is past time to blame the parents for the child's Borderline Personality Disorder in the lack of any facts or expert knowledge to support this position.

2.4: Borderline Personality Disorder is a condition that only applies to women

This isn't the case at all. In early studies of Borderline Personality Disorder, it was shown that women were negatively influenced by a 3:1 male-to-female ratio. The most recent studies have revealed that the dispersion of males and females is about identical in size. The fact that there is little information about BPD in males contributed to the myth's prevalence. One explanation for the gender disparity is that BPD testing is frequently performed in medical settings. Because women seek help more likely than men, many females with BPD are admitted to mental health institutions than men, providing the appearance that women are disproportionately affected by the disorder. Males and females must both be diagnosed and receive sufficient treatment, irrespective of sex, and this must be done in a timely manner.

BPD is a serious but curable mental health disorder. Whenever you or a member of your family has been identified with BPD and requires support, there's no safer moment to start the recovery process than now.

2.5: BPD is untreatable

With the use of DBT, trauma-centered CBT, information and communication technology, therapy, his or her resolve, the affection of family members and friends, and medication, someone no longer displays five of the BPD symptoms. As a result, he no longer falls within the DSM-5 standards for borderline personality disorder. Despite the fact that it is inconvenient, BPD can be managed, as he is live proof of.

2.6: People suffering from bipolar disorder will be unable to lead self-sufficient and satisfying lifestyles

Once a person with BPD receives the appropriate treatment, they may not be required to remain in a mental health institution perpetually. In the same way that someone with a shattered leg will begin turning up at the emergency department in need of aid if they do not receive the care they require, someone suffering from BPD will do that if they do not receive the treatment they require.

Following effective treatment, an increasing number of people are prepared to maintain their independence in order to live the lives they choose. Although they experienced some difficulties, after they received the right treatment, they were able to function on a full-time basis and attend university full-time, as well as volunteer, spend time with friends, develop healthy relationships, and pursue hobbies in their spare time.

2.7: The BPD's media-seeking activities are only a publicity stunt that may be dismissed

Impulsiveness, self-harm, and suicide ideation were all signs of depression in this case. "I don't want any attention," I didn't recall saying until I regained consciousness. In terrible mental suffering, I thought to myself, "I need assistance from my medical professionals, relatives, and friends." I awakened in excruciating emotional agony. Although I won't claim that I never acted in a way that would get attention, I did so only when I want it. The ability can save souls by devoting attention to individuals who are in distress is attainable.

It is possible to suffer a cardiac arrest or heart attack if someone who is experiencing chest tightness does not seek medical attention immediately. Individuals who are suffering from mental illness but do not seek help suffer in the same manner. After all, why should we encourage someone to suffer and ignore their agony, regardless of their medical condition? Sometimes, all it requires is 10-15 minutes of your time to listen to them and reassure someone that you love, even if you don't understand what it is they're dealing with yourself.

2.8: Patients with bipolar disorder should not attempt suicide

Because borderline personality disorder (BPD) is so misunderstood, many people who suffer from it do not receive the correct treatment. Whenever this occurs, it has the potential to lead to suicide or self-mutilating behavior. Individuals with this disorder are more likely than the general population to commit suicide or engage in self-harming behaviors. When someone commits suicide, they are in anguish, just as anybody would be if they did not try to kill themselves. Avoid rejecting it as a simple attention-seeking strategy and instead show care for the individual and investigate how you may be of support.

2.9: It is optional to be diagnosed with BPD

BPD patients will never wish to be in this state of mind. By having personal experience with depressed emotions, it is impossible to comprehend how powerful they will become. Everyone can agree that such a way of life is not something anyone would want to live in. Childhood maltreatment is a frequent contributing factor to BPD. You work in the field of behavioral health, and you've never met a person suffering from a borderline personality disorder (BPD) who had not experienced a tragic experience. So, could someone perhaps assist them in justifying their conclusion?

2.10 People suffering from bipolar disorder are unable to sustain themselves

It wasn't because you didn't want to sustain yourself when you were unwell, but rather because I couldn't. I was ill, and I lacked the financial means to provide for my medical needs. Since I was bullied as a child, I've struggled to learn how to manage my emotions. During my DBT treatment, I know how to communicate with my sadness and how to assist myself in my recovery. I was unable to heal myself for a lengthy period of time, but with time and support, I was able to accomplish it. Others will follow in their footsteps. Patients suffering from bipolar disorder (BPD) are due to time, treatment, and understanding.

2.11: Both persons who have BPD were mistreated as youngsters at some point

BPD is frequently misdiagnosed by well-intentioned persons who are unfamiliar with the disease and who believe it is triggered by a traumatic childhood experience. As a result of having BPD, others will treat you differently or talk negatively about you, which can be frustrating if you've never been mistreated. It may appear that your point of view is being misinterpreted or that your viewpoint is unique. Individuals suffering from a borderline personality disorder (BPD) have been assaulted; however, this is not indicative of all borderline personality disorder cases and should be treated with caution.

Currently, there is no proven explanation for bipolar disorder (BPD). Nevertheless, rather than being linked to a single source, the reason is typically thought to be a mixture of genetic and conservation factors at work.

2.12 Borderline personality disorder cannot be reported in childhood or teenagers

When it comes to children and adolescents, borderline personality disorder might be detected. However, because of the commonly held belief that personal growth continues during puberty, identifying adolescents or teens with BPD has grown more difficult.

Diagnostic and Statistical Manual of Mental Disorders, the Fifth Edition (DSM-V) provides detailed rules for evaluating whether or not someone has bipolar disorder. When establishing this diagnosis, extreme caution should be exercised, and this is especially true in the case of BPD because the signs and symptoms might be misinterpreted for typical teenage behavior. A professional psychiatrist with experience in bipolar disorder may be able to aid you in comparing the correlation. People who undergo therapy early in their recovery have a better chance of completing their recovery.

2.13: Borderline personality disorder (BPD) is a kind of bipolar disorder

BPD depression and borderline personality disorder are two different illnesses. Despite the fact that the symptoms of borderline personality disorder illness and borderline personality disorder are the same, they are two completely distinct diseases.

Individuals suffering from BPD are frequently misdiagnosed with bipolar illness, with four factors adding to the mystique. Additionally, many healthcare practitioners are ignorant of the disease. It's also crucial to note that medicines used to treat bipolar disease do not always work for those who have bipolar disorder. However, locating a therapist who has a history of bipolar disorder is essential for getting effective treatment and developing a treatment plan.

2.14: You don't know BPD until you meet someone who has it.

The existence of BPD would not change the reality that everyone is unique. Corresponding to the DSM-5, which serves as a guideline for mental health care, specific criteria should be met in order for BPD to be classified as such. Interpersonal functions and interpersonal interactions that are impaired are among the requirements for this diagnosis. The limitations of a person present themselves in a certain way for each individual. Furthermore, not everyone is affected by the same signals in the same way as others. Indeed, the difficulties that one individual has in relationships are not the same as yours. BPD presents itself in a number of ways depending on the individual.

2.15: Borderline Personality Disorder (BPD) is not a genuine psychological illness

In order to restrain the seriousness of the disease, the phrase BPD is frequently employed. "Borderline" implies this is a condition on the cusp of becoming a real mental illness, which is incorrect. Nerite's original purpose, on the other hand, was a way to distinguish between persons who were on the edge of neurosis and hysteria. Because borderline personality disorder (BPD) is so difficult to identify and treat, several critics have asked whether it is a distinct illness. Doctors now acknowledge borderline personality disorder (BPD) as a significant psychiatric disease and also a legitimate mental ailment.

2.16: "Support and advice complainers," who are reckless, inconsistent, and egotistical, are described as follows

Patients suffering from bipolar disorder are truly troubled and do not wish to remain in this state. Some people incorrectly believe that persons suffering from BPD are dishonest, disruptive, and potentially dangerous. People with borderline personality disorder (BPD) are frequently portrayed as violent in the media due to strong urges for rage outbursts. However, this is only one of the hundreds of BPD characteristic variants.

When someone purposefully deceives another person, they are seeking to control or influence the behavior of that person in order to attain their objectives. Because persons suffering from BPD are unable to reason their actions out and because many of their actions are driven by a deep desire for assistance, their intentions are frequently misunderstood and perceived as deceitful. Despite the fact that their behaviors appear to be planned, they frequently lack control over their emotional reactions and are unable to respond to new situations or explain themselves calmly.

The majority of specialists think that persons who suffer from BPD symptoms will be unable to physically harm others. To successfully build and maintain relationships with the proper support system of medical treatment and therapy, individuals suffering from BPD symptoms may attempt to regulate and monitor their moods and actions. Friends and family members who are empathetic and caring will assist them in accepting and connecting with anybody who has BPD and may be a part of a supportive network of people who care about them.

Everyone agrees that persons with BPD should be held accountable for their acts; alternatively, they should be held accountable for their behaviors. It will, however, be a failure if persons who suffer from BPD characteristics are dismissed as narcissistic and emotionally stable people, as some have suggested. Those experiencing BPD symptoms may feel valued, knowing that they are suffering from a legitimate medical condition, and they will be able to get the significant and necessary assistance in order to change their thought patterns.

2.17: "Treatment-resistant" and "intractable" conditions

It is tough to treat BPD patients, and it requires a high degree of participation from both the patients and those participating in the recovery process. If the services received are insufficient or poor, it may result in a substantial risk to the customer and many others in the vicinity. However, just because recovery appears to be difficult does not indicate that it is impossible. Many therapies and rehabilitation approaches have been created and examined over the last few decades, including dialectical behavior modification, which has been shown to be highly successful.

It is referred to as "emotional hypochondriacs" to characterize individuals who are suffering from empathic hypochondria, which is a form of anxiety (attention-seeking)

Temperament and suicidal tendencies are two indications of

bipolar disorder that may be misunderstood while seeking treatment. As for coping methods for dealing with emotional anguish, these self-destructive inclinations are extremely ineffective. In the majority of cases, when someone with BPD self-harms, it is done out of the public eye so that their wounds and injuries may be disguised under their clothes.

People with bipolar disorder's temper tantrums are not intended to garner attention but rather to communicate profound underlying emotions. They are not theatrical, but the more they are misunderstood, the more they fight, and the more enraged their outbursts become. It is the result of a person's behaviors being directed by emotions rather than rational thinking as a result of incorrect mental processes on his or her part. As a result, as the severity of the individual's emotional dysfunction rises, their coping technique becomes more intense, unpredictable, and impulsive in nature. As a result, any manifestation of personality disorders and depression must be treated carefully.

2.18: Being acquainted with somebody who suffers from BPD is very hard to achieve

"It is not precisely a sickness in the traditional sense."

Some persons who suffer from BPD can appear to be extremely

difficult to get along with until you offer them exactly whatever they want and require at the given moment. Both of us have a long history of studying and act in a way that has been scientifically proven in every aspect.

As a result of our formation in a stable environment, our behaviors and relationships with others are often adaptive. On the other hand, others are not so sure. Some of the ways that people with BPD have learned to act in order to get what they want from others are considered unpleasant by others with whom they speak for reasons that are out of the scope of this book.

While the specific causes of BPD are still unclear, a growing body of research shows that biology, brain function, and work, as well as climatic, social, and cultural influences, all have a part in the disease's development and progression. One thing is certain: Borderline Personality Disorder (BPD) is a very serious neurological condition that causes significant misery in individuals who suffer from this.

2.19: Patients with BPD disorder are manipulative and domineering

People facing borderline personality disorder (BPD) are frequently neglected since they are unpleasant and challenging to get along with. One possible reason for this is that persons suffering from BPD plan out how to better exploit others in order to compel them to act in particular ways, according to popular belief. It is frequently thought that the individual's chaotic, unpredictable, and inconsistent behavior is the result of a conscious decision.

The mass of people is not informed that persons suffering from bipolar disorder (BPD) are not acting in a destructive manner on purpose. It is the only way they understand how to do to take care of their own needs. Their behavioral problem causes individuals to be rigid and unyielding in their actions and reactions... It suggests that they are not aware of the existence of alternate, more adaptable behaviors that they could acquire. They switch to their old ways and do what they've previously done and what they've learned to do.

This group's efforts are driven by a desire to escape what they perceive to be a calamity worse than demise: being alone or forsaken in the wilderness. If the activity helps people to maintain the engagement of key individuals in their life, it is seen as effective and beneficial by those who participate. If they have justification for considering that someone is going to desert them, they may escalate their behaviors to whatever level is necessary to maintain control over the individual involved. For them, it is a matter of life or death at this point.

The phrase "manipulation" refers to the fact that everything was meticulously and intentionally constructed. In most cases, however, these acts are just frantic, last-ditch attempts by people suffering from bipolar disorder (BPD) to fulfill their emotional demands. They are not seeking to exert influence or exploit people of their own volition. People suffering from a borderline personality disorder (BPD) are indifferent about others around them. Simply put, they are just concerned with doing what they want. Patients with borderline personality disorder (BPD) have a difficult time managing their emotions, but this does not imply that they do not experience them. Because they can depend on other individuals to remain in their lives, they may be loving and compassionate towards others. People suffering from bipolar disorder are worried about their friends and family and are capable of feeling and expressing empathy. In spite of this, they nevertheless have a tremendous degree of sympathy towards animals.

Unfortunately, the severity of borderline personality symptoms such as mood swings, inability to connect with people, impulsive conduct, and a negative self-image is such that they can cause serious relationship problems. Someone suffering from BPD will be unable to recognize the influence of their behaviors and demands on those around them. Many people would take this as a dearth of sympathy and empathy on my part. When they understand how much grief their actions have caused other people, they may become depressed and depressed. However, the various difficulties they are coping with, particularly those pertaining to their moods, their want for affirmation, and their fear of abandonment, might make it hard for them to react to their sympathy by aiding someone else or sharing the compassion they feel with others. A huge margin of people who commit suicide does so because they are seeking assistance for their behavioral issues. They are adamant about not wanting to die at all.

Individuals are suffering from a borderline personality disorder (BPD) frequently self-harm in order to seek sympathy or evade somebody they would not want. It may also be utilized to assist people in regaining their equilibrium or in controlling their emotions. Because they may be unable to control the intensity and interpretation of their sensations, whenever they self-harm, people may be unable to control the number of discomforts they experience. It is, however, a unique sort of activity from the more traditional forms of suicidal conduct. Self-harm is frequently utilized by people suffering from BPD to damage themselves. They may think that their pain is too much for them to handle at this time and that suicide may be their only other alternative.

Many people who suffer from BPD may also be suffering from a depressive disorder, which, when combined with their impulsive and lack of mental control, can lead to lethal suicide attempts. The suicide ratio among people with BPD disorder can reach as high as 10%, and suicide is seldom the result of an accidental misinterpretation of the fatality of self-destructive behaviors. Irrespective of the severity of the deed, any form of self-harm should be taken seriously and never disregarded as a tactic to gain attention or take advantage of a situation. Self-harm, even when it is not done with the intent of harming oneself, is always destructive. There is also a definite link between non-suicidal self-harm and subsequent suicidal behavior in persons with borderline personality disorder (BPD). Even while any self-destructive conduct may be discussed, it is critical to remember that for people suffering from BPD, self-destructive behavior is largely a coping technique with a specific goal. It is essential to give the individual additional options rather than just eliminating what is believed to be a crucial component of their capacity to function in everyday life at their place of employment.

2.20: Patients with borderline personality disorder (BPD) are deadly

This belief was tragically reinforced by the film "Fatal Attraction." Persons hurting from a borderline personality disorder (BPD) are far more prone than the general public to hurt themselves. They frequently exhibit mood swings, including rage, which is regarded as undesirable and unconnected to the alleged source of the problem. Individuals can have a short fuse, get irritated for long periods of time, and even engage in violent altercations on rare occasions.

In a statistically meaningful sample taken within the United Kingdom in 2016, bipolar disorder was not shown to be associated with aggressiveness. A co-occurring condition such as borderline personality disorder or substance abuse, on the other hand, was significantly more common among individuals who had the disease, increasing the probability of anger and violence. An examination of the literature yielded a parallel result, namely, that there is no evidence that having BPD promotes aggressiveness against others on its own terms.

2.21: BPD is a personality disorder that describes a person who has a defective or bad character

Individuals have different identities, which implies they have various ways of relating to themselves, others, and the surrounding environment. Individuals who endure borderline personality disorder (BPD) may feel a substantial degree of despair in their life and relationships. A finding of borderline personality disorder does not mean that anybody is of poor character.

2.22: Dialectical behavior therapy is the most effective treatment for borderline personality disorder

DBT is an essential technique for treating borderline personality disorder. Psychotherapies such as mentalization-based psychotherapy, transference-focused treatment (TFT), and schema-focused therapy are among the most successful available (SFT). Despite significant theoretical differences, a new study found that these therapies have some common characteristics that lead to favorable outcomes for patients suffering from a borderline personality disorder.

2.23: Borderline personality disorder damages relationships

People suffering from a borderline personality disorder (BPD) may experience challenges in their interpersonal interactions, including concerns of rejection. People who suffer from BPD, on the contrary, may be able to maintain healthy, long-term relationships and overcome a significant portion of their intimacy concerns.

2.24: It is best not to disclose one's BPD condition to anybody other than one's family

When people suffering from BPD are made aware of their illness, they enjoy a sense of relief, which leads them to embrace their illnesses and circumstances. In addition, the diagnosis should aid the individual in obtaining the proper care. People suffering from borderline personality disorder (BPD) should be enlightened about the origins of their illness so that they can consider their difficulties and what therapy is helpful. In the Fact Sheet, you'll find a section titled "Providing a treatment plan for personality disorder: A guide for health providers."

2.25: When a child is under the supervision of BPD, members of the family are not always present

According to the circumstances, engaging family members and caregivers in BPD treatment may prove to be quite useful. Various family and friends are attracted to understanding more, which will aid in the correct treatment of the patient.

Chapter 3: Causes of (BPD) Borderline Personality Disorder

The Roots of Borderline Personality Disorder. The exact aetiologia of BPD, along with other psychiatric disorders, is currently unclear to researchers. There is an indication that a combination of culture (context) and environment (genetic factors or anatomy) is at work here. According to the world's leading specialists, BPD is considered to have evolved as a result of environmental, biochemical, and genetic factors. It's key to stress, though, that the specific causes of BPD are yet undetermined. Presently, these are the concepts that have received some support but are still far from being implemented. In order to understand how and why the variables listed below are associated with BPD, more research is needed.

3.1: Environmental Factors Contributing to Borderline Personality Disorder

Information indicates that there is a linkage between borderline personality disorder and stressful childhood behaviors, particularly those that involve caretakers, according to one piece of reliable evidence. Explanations of experiences that might be associated with BPD are provided below:

- Early abandonment from close members

- emotional or physical neglect

- Abuse (physical or emotional)

- Inattentiveness on the part of the parents

A mix of biological characteristics (discussed further below) and a distorted childhood environment have a part in the variables that risk someone developing borderline personality disorder (BPD). Having a kid in an intellectually invalidating environment does not allow them to meet their emotional needs. Others who have been exposed to a deceptive environment, as well as those in their immediate vicinity, are not always conscious of it. In other cases, these traumatic occurrences are disguised and even taken as praise.

People suffering from BPD do not have these kinds of childhood memories on a regular basis (even though a considerable amount have). Not everyone who goes undergone these types of situations will acquire borderline personality disorder (BPD). Rather than being caused by a single reason, the majority of borderline personality disorder claims are caused by a combination of variables.

3.2: The biological and genetic factors that contribute to Borderline Personality Disorder

Even while early research indicated that borderline personality disorder does not run in the family, it was vague for a long moment whether this was due to natural causes or heredity. There is increasing evidence that hereditary factors, as opposed to environmental ones, play a substantial role in the development of autism. Studies have discovered a link between borderline personality disorder and a variation in a gene that regulates how the brain uses serotonin (a natural chemical in the head). It appears that persons who have this serotonin gene variation are more likely to develop bipolar disorder if they have already had poor childhood behaviors (for example, abandonment from close caregivers).

According to one research, monkeys with a serotonin gene variation formed symptoms that matched those of bipolar disorder only when they were removed from their moms and placed in less safe surroundings for extended periods of time. The progression of BPD-like symptoms was significantly less likely in monkeys whose genes differed from those of their mothers, who were upraised. According to several studies, persons who suffer from BPD have differences in the shape and content of their brains. A high level of activity in brain regions that govern emotional presentation and perception has been related to borderline personality disorder (BPD). Persons with borderline personality disorder, for example, have higher concentrations of activation in the frontal lobe, which regulates aggressiveness, rage, and fear, than individuals who do not have a borderline personality disorder. It is possible that it is associated with the emotional ambiguity symptoms of BPD. Recent studies have also discovered a connection between the hormone oxytocin and the progression of BPD.

3.3: The Bottom Line on the Origins of Borderline Personality Disorder

Even though there is a great deal to understand about the causes of BPD, it is much more than likely that the illness is brought on by a combination of circumstances instead of a single issue. The investigation is still underway, and we anticipate discovering even more in the future years. People who are aware of the reasons for the illness may be able to prevent getting it, especially if they have a genetic or biological propensity to it. As things are, an annulling environment is detrimental to a kid regardless of whether it increases the chance of developing BPD in the forthcoming, and psychologists must be mindful of this scenario when working with young children.

Knowing that it be difficult to be as affirming as possible to children who have biological vulnerabilities that may lead to BPD, many words tend to be complimented, and sentiments might be easily misconstrued as the child's oversensitivity. Individuals who were psychologically invalidated as kids must learn to discern between invalidating and confirming others' statements in order to protect themselves from further injury and to handle interpersonal relationships more effectively as adults.

Contributing factors that may enhance the likelihood of developing BPD:

- Abnormalities in brain structure and function: Individuals with BPD demonstrate differences in brain structure and function, notably in the various regions of the brain that govern impulses and manage emotions. It is also unclear if these disparities are a result of developing BPD or are the result of contributing variables

- Family history of borderline personality disorder: Having parents or a sibling who suffers from BPD might raise your chances of acquiring it

- Neglect, trauma, or childhood abuse are all common childhood experiences for those who suffer from a borderline personality disorder (BPD). Many people with BPD also experienced being separated from their family members at an early age. It is important to note not everybody who gets BPD has experienced any of these childhood behaviors and that even those who have experienced them do not advance to BPD

Factors that increase the risk of developing borderline personality disorder; the likelihood of developing borderline personality disorder is increased by a number of different variables. Anyone who does not have risk factors for borderline personality disorder is not affected by it.

- Teenager or kid who has experienced physical abuse, neglect, or abandonment

- Family disturbances or relocations as a teenager or child

- Inadequate connection within the family

- Child exploitation as an adolescent or child

- Adolescent or child who has experienced sexual abuse

Borderline personality disorder has a number of complications. If borderline personality disorder consequences are left untreated or poorly managed, they can be serious or even life-threatening in difficult conditions. As part of the treatment strategy, you and your healthcare provider will devise a detailed plan to decrease the likelihood of serious consequences. There are numerous problems associated with borderline personality disorder, including:

- difficulties establishing relationships

- eating disorders

- abuse of alcohol or drugs

- Having financial or legal difficulties

- Depression, strained familial connections, self-harm, social isolation, and suicide are all possible outcomes of workplace difficulties

3.4: Etiology of BPD

Borderline personality disorder does have a number of different causes, many of which are currently unknown. There is presently no system that can include all or the majority of the data that is currently accessible. It is possible that the turning point will be genetic exposures, neurobiological and neurophysiological disorders of stressors handle, psychosocial records of childhood brutality and ill-treatment, and inconsistency of the aversive behavioral system elements (particularly the bonding system).

Genetics According to studies

Borderline personality disorder has an inheritance manipulator of 0.69; however, it is more likely that traits associated with violent emotional and behavioral, rather than BPD itself, are handed down through families. According to current research, the genetic influence on mental disorder in general, and not simply borderline personality disorder, operates both alone and in combination with aberrant environmental variables to cause mental disorder in general. Genetic investigations on cluster C anomalies have revealed that the genetic component is in between 27% and 35%, suggesting that genetic variations play a less role than previously assumed in the development of the disorder.

Neurotransmitters

Emotional control is a key issue in the treatment of borderline personality disorder. Neurotransmitters are being connected to a variety of behaviors such as impulse control, aggression, and emotion management. The neurotransmitter serotonin maintains the topic of the most extensive research and has been shown to have an adverse connection with levels of aggressiveness. Reduced serotonergic activation can make it difficult to suppress or regulate harmful impulses, although the specific process by which this occurs is yet unclear.

Environmental variables can influence the relationship between aggressiveness and 5-HT, as demonstrated by decreased 5-HT 1A (serotonin receptor) evoked responses in women who suffer from a borderline personality disorder (BPD) and a history of recurrent child abuse.

The role of catecholamines in the disruption of affective regulation is still not completely understood. When aggressiveness levels are kept under control, persons with BPD have lower amounts of free methoxy hydroxy phenyl glycol in their plasma than people who do not have the disorder. The results of administering amphetamines to persons suffering from BPD indicate that these individuals are empathetic and have greater behavioral responsiveness than the control group.

Additionally, acetylcholine, vasopressin, cholesterol, fatty acids, and the hypothalamic-pituitary-adrenal (HPA) pathway are neuromodulators and neurotransmitters that are implicated in the etiology of bipolar disorder.

Neurobiology

It has been discovered that bipolar disorder is associated with systemic and functional deficiencies in the brain regions that govern emotion, self-regulation, concentration, and working memory. The orbitofrontal and amygdala, as well as the hippocampus, are among the brain regions that have been impacted. Most research is done in the absence of an emotional stimulus. However, newer research published in the presence of an emotional challenge has shown results that are similar to those found in the absence of an emotional stimulus. Individuals suffering from BPD have greater activity in the dorsolateral prefrontal cortex and the cuneus, but the superior temporal cingulate is less active in these individuals. Observing emotionally unpleasant statements or emotional expressions has also been shown to result in greater amygdala activity, according to some research.

Psychosocial aspects of the situation

In family research, it has been observed that background of mood instability and drug misuse in other relatives, for example, may be important risk factors for BPD development. In addition, a recent study suggests that caregivers' emotional under-involvement and carelessness, which includes supervision neglect, are important factors. A prospective study in children has discovered that poor emotional participation by parents is associated with a child's psychological difficulties and, in some cases, with a higher chance of suicide. In general, people who have a borderline personality disorder (at a minimum while symptomatic) perceive their mother as overprotective or aloof and their relationship with her as conflicting, whereas their father is perceived as less active and distant. It follows that issues involving both parents, rather than problems involving only one parent, are significantly more likely to have an influence on the mutual pathogenic impact of this group. Studies of violence corroborate the general notion that biparental issues play a substantial role in the development of BPD. However, these findings need to be confirmed in persons who have recovered from the disorder.

Individuals with borderline personality disorder are more likely than the general population to experience physical, sexual, and intellectual violence in their families. Biparental neglect and emotional aggression were observed to have occurred in 84 percent of persons with BPD by 18, with caregivers' psychological denial of their involvements serving as a predictor of BPD development. That these guardians were unable to evaluate the child's point of view in light of their familial ties suggests that they were deficient in this area. It is likely that contextual elements and predisposing variables of the parent-child bond have a mediating part in the growth of BPD. In the long term, the guardian's reaction to the violence may be more important than the abuse itself... Creating a home atmosphere that discourages meaningful discussion of a kid's point of view on the world is unlikely to result in successful trauma healing. As a result, the atmosphere in which the family lives are extremely important. It has been discovered that the dysfunctional and non-nurturing environment of childhood trauma is a major social mediator of aggression and personality instability in people with bipolar disorder (BPD).

In spite of the element that first a few studies have examined how aspects of parenting and family relationships make a significant contribution to BPD vulnerability, they are the most likely component of an interpersonal system or interrupted attachment that impacts the progression of cultural cognition, which is assumed to be impaired in BPD patients.

The procedure of attachment

The body of research on the relationship between connection formation and the presence or absence of BPD is broad and conflicting. Several studies have found that early inadequate mirroring and disordered attachment, for example, can render individuals more sensitive to the time on social media interactions mentioned above, according to the researchers. This disorder is most likely associated with larger family failure, which includes rejection, neglect, excessive power, unsupportive relationships, uncertainty, and incoherence. In Spite Of the reality that there looks to be no connection between BPD diagnosis and the specific attachment category, BPD is significantly associated with the dubious connection (6-8% of

BPD clients are recognized as secure). There are symptoms of disarray in the environment (unsettled relationships and inability to understand the attachment category). Despite the data of attachment continuity from the earliest childhood minimal in adversative contexts, any person's attachment theory vulnerability is a generally persistent feature, particularly when paired with consequential adverse experiences of life (ninety-four percent). Two longitudinal studies, which followed children from birth to early adulthood, discovered a relationship between insecure attachment in young adulthood and BPD symptoms in the later years of life. Childhood connection can also play a part in the growth of borderline personality disorder. They propose that the negative consequences of disorganized or mistrust associations, which can be interrupted for a number of reasons, are arbitrated by an inability to implement the metalizing capacity – a social cognitive ability that is related to understanding and interpreting one's own and others' behavior as constructive based on constructing what is going on in the minds of one's other people.

It is comparable to the relevance of the mischaracterizing familial setting in the formation of borderline personality disorder (BPD). As a result of social separation, children have suppressed self-perceptions of cognitive states. This behavior is associated with signs of familial difficulty in the young person, as well as personal anguish and psychological difficulties, as well as components of cognitive processing, such as identifying and labeling emotion around oneself and others. A systematic weakening of a person's understanding of their own mind by the presence of alternatives and other variables results in the dynamic connection known as invalidation of that understanding. Failure to provide the individual with the ability to discriminate between their own perceptions and emotions and those of the caregiver prevents them from developing a strong metalizing skill.

Conclusion

When individuals inherit a vulnerability to social cognitive development or are subjected to external influences that stifle the development of social cognitive abilities, such as neglect in primary relationships, they develop impeded abilities to reflect on and modulate effect, as well as the ability to exert aversive governor over perceptual ability. As proven by extreme neglect, abuse, and other kinds of maltreatment, these variables can cause alterations in the neural processes of arousal and result in functional and anatomical abnormalities in the growing mind, even without additional trauma. If proper remedial measures are not implemented, the borderline personality will continue to develop.

Chapter 4: Symptoms and Likeliness of having BPD

4.1: Symptoms of Borderline Personality Disorder in General

The following are examples of signs and symptoms:

- Anxiety over losing one's position of authority

- Pervasive and deep feelings of embarrassment

- It is simple to evoke certain emotions.

- Anxiety associated with separation

- An unstable or poor sense of one's own worth and self-worth

- A high level of self-criticism

- Possessing feelings of helplessness and hopelessness

- A propensity to discount or idealize others' contributions

- Crankiness

- Depression

- Dissociative states, which occur mostly when a person is disturbed

- An inability to make decisions regarding one's objectives, aspirations, professional orientation, or basic values.

- Feelings of suicidal ideation

- Oversensitivity to imagined disapproval or judgment, particularly in the workplace

- Considered the contrast between white and black.

- Trouble adhering to or forming plans is another issue.

- It is becoming more common to be anxious or worried; to be stressed; to be concerned; to be afraid

- Persistent feelings of emptiness in the mind

- A sense of fear and unease concerning the unknown

- Taking risks via substances such as drugs and physical instability

- Feelings that are disproportionately intense in relation to the emotion's source

- Hostility

4.2: Precise Diagnosis criteria (symptoms) for BPD

Psychiatric disorders such as BPD were identified in the Diagnostic and Statistical Manual of Mental Disorders, Fifth Edition (often known as DSM-5), recognized by the American Psychiatric Association in 2013. To be identified with borderline personality disorder, you must satisfy five of the nine criteria.

Nowadays, it is common practice to divide the symptoms of the disease into four groups or domains:

A is the first domain.

Emotional comebacks are excessive, poorly controlled, and unstable.

Depression, anger, and anxiety are the most commonly experienced emotions in borderline disorder. In the DSM-5, there are nine criteria for the borderline disorder, three of which fall under this category:

1. One of the most common symptoms of affective (emotional) dysfunction is intense, episodic emotions such as anguish, anger, and panic/anxiety episodes

2. Unacceptable, strong, and difficult-to-control rage in addition to the above

3. Persistent feelings of emptiness

If you have borderline disorder, you may also experience extreme high energy ("psychological storms") or emotional response that is sometimes insufficient, as well as recurring spells of boredom and loneliness.

Domain B is comprised of the following:

Actions that are taken spontaneously are harmful to you - and others

This category covers two of the borderline disorder criteria from the DSM-5:

1. Excessive spending, dangerous and inappropriate sexual activity, binge eating, irresponsible driving, and drug misuse. Self-injurious behaviors such as striking and cutting yourself on a frequent basis are examples of suicidal thoughts, gestures, and attacks. (If you tend to cut yourself when pressured, you should consult a psychiatrist to work out why; it's a bad practice, perhaps one of the most prevalent causes is a borderline personality disorder.) You can also participate in further impulsive actions such as damaging or destroying one's own or another's property or the property of others.

Domain C

Individuals who have inaccurate opinions of others and themselves are more likely to be dishonest.

This category covers two of the borderline disorder criteria from the DSM-5:

1. A self-image or sense of self that is distinctively and continuously imbalanced (your perceptions of your identity and of yourself)

2. Suspicion of others' opinions of you, and even deluded ideation, or transient and stress-associated dissociation episodes in which you perceive yourself or your environment as unreal

There are symptoms in this Domain such as "all-or-nothing" or divided thinking, difficulty "pulling" your thoughts together so that they make sense, and rational issue resolution, particularly in social disagreements, to name a few.

Domain D

Ultimately, you may find yourself in relationships that are uncontrolled and extremely imbalanced.

The final two DSM-5 criteria are included in this category:

1. You may make frantic efforts to avoid being abandoned, whether the abandonment is real or imagined

2. It is possible that your relationships will be passionate and destructive, with you alternately idealizing and undervaluing those who are important to you

In addition, you will find that you tend to be too reliant and clinging in major relationships. Moreover, you may have high anticipation of bad and harmful attitudes and actions from the majority of others, and you may have difficulty thinking clearly in difficult social situations, as well.

Chapter 5: Relating Experiences of BPD

Broadening your understanding of BPD by understanding what diagnosed patients go through on average can really help you. Here are some people talking about their life with BPD.

I NEED TO LIVE IN THE MOMENT. BUT WHICH MOMENT....

5.1: Unknown Individual

"I have BPD. I get paranoid easily. I go through abandonment problems at times. I'm super impulsive. I change my mind too often. I feel emotions more intensely than others. I have a super intense emotional response. Often, I need to receive reassurance on certain things. I get furious or upset more quickly, comparatively speaking.

I seek acceptance almost all the time. I do work hard to lessen the symptoms, but BPD is something I will always have to deal with. It's uncontrollable. Nevertheless, I am a loyal friend. A loyal partner. I care for the people I love. Compassionate. Funny. Empathetic. Strong. A lot of fun.

If you cannot accept me, you are the one missing out. I am not ashamed of my disorder, and neither should you."

5.2: A Facebook User

"Sometimes, BPD kills your motivation to even move. It's like it's physically impossible to do absolutely anything productive. Simultaneously, not doing anything causes guilt. Then the chain reaction begins. Guilt causes stress and anxiety. Stress and extreme anxiety cause deep despair. Then the deep recession? Causes a serious lack of energy. Severe lack of energy leads to the death of motivation and prevents you from doing productive activities. A horrible and vicious BPD cycle."

5.3: Anonymous

"There's just such a broad spectrum of the ways in which the disorder presents itself. 9 traits. You will have at least 5 of the 9 to receive a diagnosis. On the other hand, having 5 or more means, there are just too many diverse combinations of BPD leading to different ways the traits can manifest. So you either have borderline who works well daily, doesn't take any medication, never admitted to the hospital, or borderline who has been admitted to the hospital for 6 years, is addicted to drugs and struggles with the community/society. BPD is unique to each person who suffers from good and bad days."

5.4: A Survivor

"Borderline Personality Disorder is the only psychological disorder where the patient is expected to "control" themselves since they still have "free will" and are still "responsible" for their symptoms. I knew someone who said that someone spitting on them was abuse. That's literally a symptom of the illness. If someone does not have the resources available to get help or the disorder capacity is larger than their will to conform to the normalcy, sometimes people with this diagnosis really genuinely actually can't control their reaction to things.

Individuals with BPD have a minute capability in the prefrontal cortex, hippocampus, and amygdala that regulates emotional reactions and impulses. It's not some pseudo psychic internalization of trauma. It is a genuine disorder, and you cannot pick and choose what symptoms you prejudice."

5.6: A Feeler

"I feel too much. Love too much. Care too much. Want too much. Give too much. Isolate too much. Need too much. Get scared too much. Get insecure too much. Get nervous too much. Get triggered too much. Stay awake too much. Am bothered too much. Absorb too much. Push people away too much. Criticize me too much. Overthink too much. Apologize too much. Worry too much.

Today feels too much for anyone and everyone."

5.7: What I Learnt

"What I learned in 2020?

- Comparing your body to others will never make you happy. The one thing it does is prevent you from seeing the beauty you radiate.

- Take time for yourself; it's never selfish. It's vital.

- Set boundaries. You never need to say yes to everything.

- Hang to basics. Walk. Sleep. Read. Hydrate.

- Inform your friends and family that you love them. You never know when you'll see them.

- Devote your time doing the events you revel in. They will never fail to bring you joy.

Never forget to share your positivity for someone else once in a while."

5.8: The Reminder

"Shout out to the people with borderline whose generosity has been exploited.

Shout out to those with BPD who have been used countless times due to how loyal they are.

Shout out to those with BPD who never fail to dedicate themselves entirely to that person and can't experience the same dedication.

Shout out to those with BPD who get abandoned because their people don't have the mental capacity to reciprocate the level of emotions they experience.

Shout out to those with BPD who can't really establish friendships due to abandonment issues.

Shout out to you; you are not alone."

5.9: What it Feels like?

"Having BPD feels like you have two personalities in you. You shove all that trauma and abuse into one little area of yourself for the longest time, and it metastasized and grew until it took over one entire personality. Now? You're continuously at war with the personality you hate, but still, you cannot help but empathize with the monster. You are fully aware it's only the product of all the pain you fed it.

Having BPD, having two souls. One it malicious and cruel and so hateful. The other is genuine and loving and so kind. But your body doesn't have room for both, so you battle between decisions on which is yours."

5.10: What I Must Learn as a BPD sufferer?

"Things I'm still trying my best to learn:

- Failure often leads to insight.

- Struggling doesn't equal failure.

- Say "no". It's self-care.

- The healing process is often never linear.

- Self-compassion is necessary in times of growth/transition.

- It's helpful to provide space for your mind and body to regenerate.

- Your worth is never up for debate.

- Having boundaries is vital.

Growth can sometimes look like annihilation. Keep that in mind."

5.11: BPD Splitting

"Among the most struggling symptoms is to deal with "splitting". To the core, it is the tendency to see things as black and white when you're upset. For instance, having a favorite person, which is a word used for someone who a person with mental illness is close to and relies on. Usually, the person with a mental disorder idealizes their favorite person to a limit. The splitting happens when the favorite person does something wrong, as humans do. Even something simple like being late for a meeting or making a comment that hurt the person with BPD. At that moment, the favorite persons' level goes from a high horse to living in the gutter."

5.12: The Poet

"There are stars you've not yet seen,

Loves you haven't yet loved,

Light's you haven't yet felt,

Sunrises yet to dawn,

Dreams you haven't yet dreamt,

Days you haven't yet lived,

Nights you won't yet forget,

Flowers you haven't yet picked,

There is more to you that you haven't yet seen."

5.13: Chimere

"Please. Text first. Tell me every single little detail about your day. Tell me you're proud. Tell me before leaving. Don't leave. Tell me when you're busy. Don't think I'm crazy. Don't look at me. Please."

5.14: Scream to the Night

"I would never wish BPD on anyone. Except if you have it, there is no way to explain that feeling that boils in you when you witness or hear something you really didn't want to. It's like at that moment, the only thing that can make you feel better is ripping your skin off, laying in the dirt and screaming into the sky, or killing yourself. Every day is a nightmare. I'm tired."

5.15: Misunderstood

"Release yourself from the expectations of people to be a certain way just because you are. You have a big heart with a deep soul. Most won't understand or respect that. Let go of the desire of wanting to be understood and flow in your self-love. Who and what will be in your life will unfold itself?"

5.16: Imaginary Life

"I think among the worst symptoms of BPS is the lack of

emotional permeance. No matter how many amazing and caring people you are close to, the moment you are left alone, it's like you were never loved that it was just all in your head. Creation of your imagination."

5.17: A Meaningful Conversation

"My therapist told me something meaningful. He said, "It is vital to keep in mind that once you're depressed, you have to nurse yourself and be very gentle towards yourself. Just as a runner wouldn't break an ankle, then force themselves to sprint with that ankle. The rest recovers and never thinks, "I am a failure runner". Instead, they think, "Now, something wasn't working, so I'll just take care of myself until it does."

Just like a broken limb, depression can alter the way your daily life plays out, and push yourself harder and getting furious and irritated when you don't feel better is exactly like attempting to sprint on a broken ankle and getting irritated when it doesn't. Heal."

5.18: Abandonment

"When it comes to psychology, the fear of abandonment is a complicated phenomenon that is considered to have its roots in childhood loss or trauma. This dread has been investigated from a number of different viewpoints. Theories on why the fear of abandonment develops in young children include disruptions in the normal development of their social and mental skills, prior relationships and personal experiences, and exposures to certain norms and beliefs.

In spite of the truth that it is not officially recognized as fear, the phobia of loneliness is one of the most common and most dangerous worries that people have. The fear of abandonment can lead to obsessive actions and thinking patterns that damage one's ability to maintain healthy relationships, ultimately leading to the abandonment that one fears becoming a reality. This kind of worry may be crippling. -the highly clear and concise mind

Abandonment Can Be Caused by a Conflict:

There are various ways in which this is a double-whammy. People with borderline personality disorder (BPD) are both afraid of abandonment and exhibit characteristics that create friction with others and frequently result in rejection, which then feeds the anxiety. Furthermore, persons suffering from BPD are prone to be particularly sensitive to the sensation of being abandoned. Consequently, even though the ending of a partnership is difficult for everyone, the termination of a relationship may be particularly traumatic for those suffering from bipolar disorder.

Methods for Breaking the Toxic Cycle of Violence and Abandonment include:

However, the great news is there are activities you may do in order to try to break this vicious cycle. For instance, in dialectical behavior therapy (DBT), a set of abilities known as the "interpersonal effectiveness" skills is taught to the clientele. These abilities can assist you in becoming more effective in your relationships, which can result in those connections becoming stronger and much more likely to last. If you are not already receiving DBT, it might be something you should discuss with your therapist.

It is also possible that schema-focused therapy will be beneficial in recognizing and actively altering harmful patterns of thinking that are causing problems in your life. Identifying unmet needs that you have been attempting to get everyone else to satisfy in an unhealthy manner will assist you in identifying healthy methods to meet those needs and finding healthy ways to have those needs filled."

5.19: Emotional Dysregulation

"What emotional dysregulation really is, and how does it manifest itself?

When an individual is unable to manage their impulses in the same manner as others, this is referred to as emotional dysregulation. Their emotions are very strong, and they are unable to control them even after they have calmed down and used appropriate coping strategies.

In times of emotional stress, people who have excellent emotion regulation abilities are able to resist the desire to engage in impulsive actions such as self-harm, official misconduct, or physical violence. This is known as the "well-mind."

An illustration of the difference between Emotion Regulation and Dysregulation

Example: If somebody who doesn't have BPD has a breakup, she is likely to be sad and may even be a little depressed, but she's also able to regulate her emotions and go about her daily routine without being overwhelmed. She will continue to attend class and work as usual. Someone suffering from BPD, on the other hand, is unable to control their emotions in a healthy manner. A repeat of the same scenario may cause him to get depressed and suicidal of not functioning, which may manifest itself in destructive or aggressive conduct, as well as impulsive activities like prostitution and other vices. Managing Emotions is a skill.

While BPD disorder makes emotion control challenging, it is not impossible to attain this ability and recover from a borderline personality disorder.

Seeing a borderline personality disorder specialist may be beneficial if you are struggling with BPD and emotions. They will need a superior sense of the underlying issues that are contributing to your emotional difficulties. You and your partner may collaborate on developing methods to help you better manage your emotions.

Mental, behavioral therapy and dialectic behavior therapy are two types of psychotherapy that have been shown to be particularly helpful for entities hurting from a borderline personality disorder.

Therapy has a lot to offer in terms of benefits. It will educate you on how to identify and monitor your mood fluctuations in a healthy way. Over time, your ability to regulate your emotions will increase, which will benefit you in both your interpersonal interactions and your everyday life.

In addition to treatment, there are a number of self-help techniques for bipolar disorder that may help you improve your capacity to control your emotions even more effectively."

5.20: Real Talk

"When are you going to seriously begin telling your friend's REAL advice? Something like, 'Hey! You're amazing, but you do need to go for therapy'. 'Hey, I care about you and what you do to yourself isn't healthy, and you need to face your hardships head-on. 'Hi, I am with you throughout, but I can't support the bad habits you've created."

5.21: Self-harming

"Self-Mutilation is due to a variety of factors; many individuals think that individuals who self-mutilate do it in order to attract attention. This is a fallacy. The majority of individuals who self-harm do so in secret, and they take care to conceal any signs or scars that result. They will often wear long sleeves in order to conceal these indications. They are often embarrassed by their actions and want to keep them hidden. Those suffering from BPD who are sensitive to rejection, in particular, are always concerned about others finding out what they are hiding from them.

Several studies have shown that the majority of individuals who self-mutilate do so in order to assist manage internal experiences such as strong emotions, ideas, memories, and body reactions, among other things.

Who is it that commits self-mutilation?

Sadly, self-mutilation is a frequent occurrence, especially among individuals suffering from bipolar disorder. According to one research, about 40 percent of college students had participated in self-mutilation at least once, with approximately 10 percent had engaged in self-mutilation ten or more times throughout their lives. According to the evidence, males and females allow for self-harm at about the same rates.

Self-mutilation is more common among people who have suffered mistreatment during their upbringing, such as physical abuse and neglect, or who have been removed from a caregiver throughout their youth. This is especially true for those who are mentally ill."

5.22: Sense of Self

"Do you frequently find yourself pondering, "Who am I?" or "What am I doing here?" What is it that I believe in? What exactly is my position in this world? If this is the case, you are not alone. Many individuals who suffer from BPD deal with identity problems, which is one of the main symptoms of BPD-The very well mind, according to the National Institute of Mental Health.

Understanding One's Own Identity:

Identities, according to the majority of experts, are defined as your overall perspective and perception of yourself. A solid sense of identity refers to the ability to perceive oneself as the same individual in the old days, today, and tomorrow. It is important to maintain this ability. Also necessary for maintaining an unwavering sense of self is the capacity to see oneself in a consistent light, regardless of the fact that you may sometimes behave in conflicting ways.

Identity is a wide concept that encompasses many different elements of one's personality. If you have a positive sense of identity or identity, it is most likely comprised of your ideas, emotions, skills; history; ways of acting; personality; temperament, knowledge, views, and roles, and so on. Identity may be regarded as your consciousness; it is the glue that binds all of these disparate parts of yourself — including your very good mind — together in one place.

Why Do People With Borderline Personality Disorder Have Identity Issues?

Regrettably, there has been little study on the identity issues linked with borderline personality disorder (BPD), even though there are more than a few theories as to wherefore individuals with BPD often suffer from their identities. One prominent BPD scientist and the creator of dialectical behavior therapy (DBT), Marsha Linehan, Ph.D., thinks that you create an identity through monitoring your own emotions, ideas, and experiences, as well as the responses of others to you and your conduct. In the case of BPD, as well as the accompanying emotional instability, impulsive conduct, and dichotomous thinking, it is possible that you may have difficulties in developing a cohesive sense of self since your internal feelings and outward behaviors will be inconsistent.

In addition, many individuals who suffer from BPD originate from a turbulent or violent upbringing, which may lead to their fragile sense of self and identity. If you decide whom you are based on the responses of people to you, and even those responses have been unexpected and/or frightening, you will have no foundation for establishing a strong sense of personal identity in the future."

5.23: My Emptiness

"My disease, BPD, has many criteria for a diagnosis, one of which is a persistent sensation of "emptiness," which I feel most strongly. I placed the term "emptiness" in quotes since, as I and those who suffer from a borderline personality disorder (BPD) know, the sensation is not precisely "emptiness," which suggests a blank or vacuum where it should be.

Yes, there is a certain aspect of feeling that something is lacking inside myself, which may lead to a great deal of reaching out of myself for security and identity, as well as sometimes frantic efforts to bridge an intellectual, mental, or religious chasm. This has shown itself in my own history via a series of job changes, housing moves, and relationship changes — as well as tense eating habits (using physical fullness as a stand-in for soul fullness). However, when I reflect on the persistent emotion that was at the root of all of these harmful behaviors, I believe that yearning may be a more appropriate word than emptiness. It is not just the apparent absence but also the desire for it to be done with joy, connection, and satisfaction that drives this yearning. Many people have the urge to "figure out" what that means - whether we represent as individuals, what we signify as a species, and what we represent as sentient creatures in a vast and incomprehensible world. The distinction is that having borderline personality disorder intensifies the desire, making it deeper and more constant than it would otherwise be.

However, despite the fact that the constant, nagging, empty presence may be draining and can lead people to reckless and self-destructive behavior, it is the environment in which many of us tiny BPD fish find ourselves. In reality, my own therapist and many other health professionals who deal with BPD patients have praised their profound philosophical insights and unique ability to explore the meaning of life and one's own identity as a result of their treatment. Whenever anyone comes to me with feelings of alienation from a purpose, or with doubts about what really gives pleasure and fulfillment, or just with tears in their eyes because they are hungry for something that is difficult to express, I can help them find their way. Because I have come to terms with emptiness and come to terms with longing— The All-Powerful."

Chapter 6: BPD and Other Overlapping Conditions

6.1: Addiction

Overlap

This is referred to as the overlap Between Borderline Personality Disorder and Addiction

In certain cases, it may be difficult to distinguish between addiction and borderline personality disorder (BPD) when they occur together since the symptoms of both illnesses are so similar. When a person displays antisocial and manipulative characteristics, the therapy process may be especially difficult to complete. This is referred to as the overlap. Both are characterized by self-destructive and impulsive behaviors. Mood swings, ranging from severe depression to psychotic episodes of great severity, may be seen in both cases of bipolar disorder and schizophrenia.

Deceptive and manipulative behavior distinguishes the two types of behavior.

A lack of regard for own safety and health may be characterized as a disregard for one's own life as well as persistence in participating in hazardous activities despite the risks associated with such activities.

In both instances, there is a general tendency toward insecurity in relationships, work, and financial situations.

Indications of drug or alcohol addiction include suicidal thoughts, irritability, sadness, and anxiety, among others. Because of this, managing a Dual Diagnosis such as this at a traditional treatment facility may be difficult. In order to accept BPD as a simultaneous illness, the institution must offer patients with customized treatment programs for their dual diagnosis.

In accordance with the publication Addiction Science & Clinical Practice, the therapy goals of dual diagnosis treatment for DBT include the following:

- Assisting the client in discovering the motivation to make major changes in their lives.

- Individuals may learn how to regulate their emotions and deal with triggers via the use of technical skills like mindfulness meditation, for example.

- It is necessary to eliminate the social and environmental cues that promote drug addiction.

- Taking away a person's desire to consume alcohol or engage in drug usage

- Making a conscious effort to identify and participate in

meaningful, self-affirming activities that promote a feeling of belonging

- Assistance in establishing and attaining realistic treatment objectives, like staying clean for a period of 24 hours on end, for the client.

Integrated care clients participate in preventative care programs and rehab sessions in relation to personal treatment for borderline personality disorder (BPD). Recognizing that relapse is a significant risk in Dual Diagnosis treatment, effective preventative care training is essential. When dealing with borderline personality disorder and addiction, clients are often encouraged to participate in support groups where they may discuss coping strategies and confront the difficulties of co-occurring disorders.

Once you have a personality condition such as Borderline Personality Disorder (BPD), which affects your interpersonal interactions and emotions, therapy and counseling are not always sufficient treatment options.

The use of drugs to treat addiction, including those used to treat mental illness, maybe useful therapeutic tools when they are incorporated into a comprehensive treatment strategy. If a patient is suffering from BPD, a medication that is intended to restore neurotransmitter balance may be of assistance to them, and this would include antidepressants of the selective serotonin reuptake inhibitor class. Additional anti-addiction medicines like Suboxone and Naltrexone are available to assist/reduce withdrawal symptoms while also decreasing the urge for alcohol and opiate substances, according to the National Institute on Drug Abuse.

Addiction and borderline personality disorder (BPD) may be treated simultaneously at rehabilitation facilities that offer dual diagnosis treatment to their patients. Patients may benefit from these services since they can get both psychotherapy and substance addiction treatment. At the rehab facility, they are exposed to a variety of therapeutic approaches, such as spatial cognition therapy, that are designed to help patients comprehend the thought processes that lead to their impulsive conduct. Treatment with cognitive behavioral therapy helps patients gain more control over their emotions and is less likely to result in self-medication with alcohol or drugs.

For instance, according to one study, individuals suffering from borderline personality disorder accounted for 40% of those seeking buprenorphine to aid in the treating of opiate addiction. A background of med pain misuse is reported by about 50% of individuals with borderline personality disorder (BPD) (about 9.2%). More than half of individuals who had a lifetime diagnostic for BPD also had a documented substance abuse problem in the previous 12 months, according to separate research; similarly, the study showed that 9.5% who had an ongoing lifelong addiction also had time to resolve for BPD. Once again, a long-term study revealed that 60% of people with BPD qualified for drug addiction when the research started; however, after 10 years of follow-up, 90% of these people had retained abstinence for at least a time period, which is considered to be withdrawal of the addiction in this case.

In contrast, individuals with BPD, even while they had complete remission over the decades after the study's completion, were more likely to relapse into their addiction than other people. Approximately 40% of research subjects returned to alcohol use disorder, with a further 35% relapsing into substance abuse disorder. Only 21% of the participants acquired a new addition to a substance, while 23% got a new alcohol addiction. There were no new or distinct addictions discovered in the group.

When it comes to substance misuse among individuals with borderline personality disorder, tobacco and booze are the most often abused. In the US, the era prevalence of nicotine addiction (often smoking) is about 57%, while the life frequency of alcohol addiction is 64%.

The signs of BPD include hazardous and impulsive actions, as well as strong moods or emotions. As an end result, it is more likely that a person suffering from BPD would acquire addictions or drug abuse issues than in the other way around.

Drug addiction, on the other hand, may precipitate BPD, and drug addiction will exacerbate BPD.

One of the most difficult challenges for those attempting to determine the connection between the two illnesses is that drug abuse may significantly exacerbate the symptoms of BPD, such as mental instability, recklessness, and personality problems. In addition, there is a higher risk of suicide attempts, shorter abstinence periods, and a higher rate of treatment dropouts. As a result, the treatment of bipolar disorder in conjunction with a drug addiction needs a unique therapeutic strategy.

Unlike the general population, BPD and drug use illnesses have an early start, with younger individuals experiencing greater rates of comorbidities than the general public. Age is not a contributing factor to either disease; nevertheless, childhood trauma is a common characteristic across both.

Some evidence suggests that drug use disorders may lead to BPD or that BPD can lead to substance use disorders. For example, prolonged drug usage may lower serotonin levels, resulting in disinhibition, self-destructive, and impulsive behavior in certain individuals. Individuals who are neuro-biologically vulnerable to BPD are more sensitive to the consequences of drug addiction than the general population. Examples include drug addiction, which may result in the loss of key relationships as well as other life stresses, which can ultimately lead to BPD in susceptible populations.

Some people with BPD, on the other hand, may resort to psychoactive drugs such as opioids, cocaine, or alcohol in order to self-medicate the overpowering symptoms of emotional distress, and this reliance may progress to drug addiction over time. Opiates, whether in naturally derived form, are pain relievers, and 18.5 percent of individuals with bipolar disorder misuse opiates to alleviate the symptoms of anger or aggressiveness. Mood and confidence are elevated, tiredness is reduced, and energy and productivity are increased as a result of cocaine use. BPD is diagnosed in about 16.8 percent of individuals who are addicted to cocaine. Drug users often want to alleviate emotions such as emptiness, boredom, depressed moods, or restlessness by using cocaine. Alcohol is abused by about 14.3 percent of people suffering from BPD because it is a sedative that soothes and relaxes stiff emotional discomfort, causing consumers to be in disengaged moods.

As previously stated, the rate of present drug use among people with BPD is 14 percent, while the prevalence of lifetime substance use among those with BPD is 78 percent. There is an obvious connection stuck between drug use disorder and borderline personality disorder, and being aware of this connection can help to ensure that individuals who suffer from co-occurring illnesses get proper treatment and care.

Seeking professional assistance

Early diagnosis for both borderline personality disorder and drug use problems should be approached in a hierarchical fashion. Patients with alcohol dependency and concomitant bipolar disorder benefit from open communication for the symptoms of substance addiction to the same degree as alcoholic patient's dependence and bipolar disorder alone. Patients with drug dependency should be treated with care, according to recent research, which showed that prescription substance misuse is equally prevalent in both men and females with bipolar disorder. The most successful treatment for both illnesses is to get them from therapists who have a continuously good mindset of acceptance and high competence in both diseases and who can provide distinct skill development and socio-therapy for each disorder at the same time.

6.2: BPD with Eating Disorders

Dietary habits and borderline personality (BPD) are often associated with one another, but until recently, little was understood about the nature of the connection between the two. According to a recent study, BPD and anorexia disorders co-occur on a regular basis, and there may be a link between the two. Scientists are also discovering more about how to cope with these two kinds of illnesses once they do co-arise.

So what are the Symptoms of Eating Disorders?

Eating disorders are mental illnesses defined by significant difficulties with eating behavior, as well as thoughts and feelings associated with eating behavior and eating disorders. Eating disorders are classified into eight categories according to the Diagnostic and Statistical Manual of Mental Illnesses, Fifth Edition (DSM-5), which is the standard guideline for the identification of psychiatric disorders used among health professionals. The following eating disorders are listed in the DSM-5:

- Anorexia nervosa

- Consumption disorder characterized by avoidance or restriction of food consumption (ARFID)

- Anorexia is a kind of eating problem that occurs when a

person consumes an excessive quantity of nutrition in a short time

- Bulimia nervosa is an eating condition that involves the psyche and body.

- Disorder of ruminating

- Additional eating or feeding disorders that have been identified (OSFED)

- Pica

- Feeding or eating problem that has not been identified (UFED)

Anorexia nervosa and Bulimia

Anorexia nervosa is characterized by excessive dietary restriction, a concern with weight gain, and a severely reduced body weight.

Bulimia nervosa is exemplified by the occurrence of binge eating, which is followed by behaviors that are intended to counteract the eating disorders, such as self-induced vomit, misuse of laxatives, exercising excessively, and others.

In certain cases, the symptoms of these two diseases are similar to one another. Someone may, for example, indulge in binge eating while simultaneously refusing to maintain healthy body weight.

Binge Eating Disorder

A kind of eating disorder occurs when a person consumes excessive amounts of food in a short period of time. In 2013, the DSM included binge-eating disorder as a diagnosis. The disease is characterized by bouts of binge eating during which individuals believe that they are losing control over their food. Feelings of shame or guilt are often experienced as a result of these occurrences. In contrast to bulimia, there have been no compensatory behaviors associated with anorexia. There are many treatment options for Binge Eating disorders.

Eating Disorders that Aren't Listed Above

Pica and rumination disease was transferred from the now-defunct DSM-IV part of disorders often diagnosed in infancy, youth, and adolescence to the eating and dieting section of the DSM-5.2. Pica and rumination disease were formerly classified as eating disorders in the DSM-IV.

Pica is characterized by the desire for and ingestion of non-food items. Rumination disorder is characterized by the regurgitation of previously consumed food to spit it out or re-allow it.

Avoidant/restrictive eating behavior disorder is a new

diagnosis in the Diagnostic and Statistical Manual of Mental Disorders (DSM). It was formerly called a partial eating disorder. This condition is characterized by a restriction in calorie consumption, but it is not accompanied by anxiety about one's weight or concern about weight growth or loss.

"Other defined" and "undisclosed" umbrella diagnosis possibilities are also included in the DSM-5 for diseases that do not satisfy the diagnostic criteria for other eating disorders, such as binge-eating disorder or anorexia nervosa.

Occurrence

A greater prevalence of eating disorders is seen in individuals who have borderline personality disorder as compared to people in the population.

For instance, conducted highly recognized research in which they discovered that 53.8 percent of patients with a borderline personality disorder also fulfilled the criteria for an eating problem (compared to 24.6 percent of clients with other personality disorders).

According to the findings of this research, 21.7 percent of patients with BPD highest ratio for anorexia nervosa and 24.1 percent met the criteria for bulimia nervosa, respectively.

Of course, this does not imply that individuals suffering from eating problems are also suffering from a borderline personality disorder. In truth, the massive mass of individuals who endure eating problems does not have bipolar illness.

When comparing individuals with eating disorders to the general population, it seems that the incidence of BPD is somewhat higher—approximately 6 percent to 11 percent, compared to 2 percent to 4 percent in the overall population—which suggests that BPD is more prevalent in this group.

Some eating disorders, on the other hand, are linked with a greater chance of developing BPD than others. According to one research, individuals who suffer from bulimia nervosa, purging type, may be at higher risk for BPD (with about 11 percent fulfilling BPD criteria) than people who suffer from anorexia nervosa, binge-eating/purging type (with about 4 percent meeting BPD criteria).

Contrary to popular belief, borderline personality disorder does not need medication.

What Is the Relationship Between Them?

Why do individuals with borderline personality disorder (BPD) appear to have eating problems at a higher incidence than the overall population? One potential reason, according to experts, is that BPD and food disorders (especially bulimia nervosa) have a similar risk factor, which they have identified.

A record of childhood abuse, such as bodily, sexual, or emotional abuse, is linked with both borderline personality disorder and eating disorders.

A history of traumatic experiences may put a person at higher risk for both bipolar illness and eating problems, according to some researchers.

As an additional point of consideration, some experts have indicated that the signs of BPD may put a human at heightened risk of forming an eating problem. For example, persistent impulsivity and impulses to self-harm may contribute to the development of problematic eating behaviors that, if left untreated, may progress to the degree of an eating disorder over time.

Individuals who are genetically predisposed to BPD may suffer stress as a result of participating in eating disordered behavior (e.g., severe shame, hospitalization, and family disturbance), which may result in the onset of BPD in those who are not predisposed.

Treatments

What can be done to treat borderline personality disorder and co-occurring anorexia nervosa? For both kinds of diseases, the great news is there are effective therapies available. However, although some research has shown that individuals with BPD do not react as well to eating disorder therapy as those without BPD, other studies have found that there is no difference in patients treated between people with anorexia and those who do not have BPD.

Which of the following problems should be addressed first? However, it is possible to treat both an eating problem and the symptoms of BPD illness at the same time; however, this will be determined on an individual basis. Example: Some individuals have binge eating signs that are so extreme that they are instantly life-threatening, while others do not.

As a result, hospitalization for the disordered eating problems may be required prior to treatments for the BPD symptoms may be started. The BPD symptoms may also be addressed initially in the case of someone who has very strong BPD indicators that are otherwise life-threatening or that are threatening to impair their ability to participate in the treatment program.

Anorexia may arise when a person develops a regular practice of eating that is triggered by emotional hunger rather than by physiological hunger. As a result, rather than relying on our internal hunger signals (physical desire) to guide our eating habits, emotions (emotional hunger) frequently grab the wheel, influencing our urge to consume food. Depending on the person, different emotions — anxiety, boredom, anger, frustration, irritability, and so on — can either increase one's appetite and cause one to consume more or decrease appetite and cause one to consume less food.

It is critical for those suffering from an eating disorder to learn appropriate methods to self-soothe through times of distress, dysregulation, and disturbance, as well as how to eat when physically hungry rather than when emotionally hungry, as part of their treatment. Often important in the healing process is instinctive eating, also called mindful eating or mindful eating as a technique. Using instinctive eating, people re-learn how to accept his/her own body, enabling him/them to eat whatever they want and whenever they choose by following inner hunger and fullness signals.

If you think you could be struggling from an eating problem, there is help available for you to get well. Possessing the skills, help, and tools you need for your path may assist you on your road to recovery as well as keep your recovery on track.

No matter how serious the dilemma, you could indeed recoup from anorexia and live a pleased and enjoyable life, liberate the discomfort and worry associated with food. You will learn to eat fluidly whilst also exemplifying a healthy balanced diet, as well as self-acceptance and gratefulness for your body once you have recovered from an eating disorder.

When compared to controls, adolescents with BPD had substantially higher disturbed eating behavior. Eight of the nine aspects of borderline personality disorder were shown to be strongly associated with disordered eating, indicating that there is significant shared variation between the categories of BPD and eating disorders. According to the findings of this book, the rejection sensitivity of the participants substantially moderated the connection between BPD signs and eating disorders behavior.

One thing to examine would be that the eating problem or borderline personality disorder should be addressed first. In many cases, this is determined on a case-by-case situation, based on whether some of the unhealthy lifestyle or BPD signs are potentially fatal, and then by determining how they connect with each other.

There are a variety of therapy methods available for BDP, which are often also effective for treating eating disorders as well. Behavioral therapy (DBT), schema therapy, and mentalization-based therapy are examples of such treatments (MBT).

6.3: Depression with BPD

A large number of individuals who suffer from a borderline personality disorder (BPD) as well struggle with depressive symptoms. In fact, it is extremely rare for BPD and sadness not to occur together. But what makes depression in BPD different from other types of depression, and how could having both illnesses impact your treatment options?

What Is the Definition of Depression?

Depression is a general word that does not refer to a particular illness. Depressed (low) mood, on the other hand, is referred to by this word. Depression is a mind that goes beyond regular sorrow. Several mental health illnesses, such as mood disorders and schizoaffective disorder (a psychosis disorder that involves mood symptoms), as well as some personality disorders, may contain aspects of depression (such as BPD).

When someone has one or even more periods of sad mood, he or she may be labeled with major depression or another illness, depending on whether or not additional symptoms are present at the same time.

Persons suffering from bipolar disorder (which is frequently confused with BPD) may, for example, experience both periods of low mood and episodes of elevated mood (mania and may be diagnosed with bipolar disorder. Depression may also manifest itself in other ways, such as dysthymic disorder (which is characterized by chronic, low concentrations of depressed mood). Depression may occur outside of these disease criteria as well, for example, in the aftermath of a loss.

There is a very high incidence of comorbidities among borderline personality disorder (BPD) and depression, which indicates that many individuals who have BPD also have issues with depressed mood.

BPD and Depression: The Scope of the Problem

According to one research, about 96 percent of individuals with BPD fulfilled the treatment guidelines for a mood illness. Patients with borderline personality disorder fulfilled the criteria for major depressive disorder in this study, while patients with borderline personality disorder signal obtained for dysthymic disorder in this research.

Is Depression Treated Differently in Borderline Personality Disorder?

Many specialists have observed that depression often manifests itself in a different way in individuals with BPD than those who do not have the disorder. As a result, depression in BPD has been described as having a different quality than depression in general. For instance, whilst depressive symptoms are strongly correlated with unhappiness or remorse, depression in BPD has indeed been described as being associated with feelings of resentment, deep shame (feeling emotionally like a bad and evil person), loneliness, and emptiness.

When sad, people with borderline personality disorder (BPD) often report feeling extremely bored, restless, and/or painfully lonely. Depressing periods in individuals with borderline personality disorder (BPD) are often caused by interpersonal losses, as well (like a breakup of a relationship).

What Role Does Borderline Personality Disorder Play in Depression Treatment?

Patients who have both a temperament disorder and depression had worse reactions to therapy than those who do not have a personality problem, according to pretty convincing data. Individuals with personality disorders and depression have poorer responses to treatment, according to a meta-analysis of research that investigated treatment outcomes in people with PDs and depression. The great news is that study has shown that if a client with BPD and depression is handled for BPD and sees progress in those, the person with BPD and depression will see improvement in that s as well. This impact seems to only be effective in one way (for instance, treatment focused mainly on the depression symptoms doesn't seem to increase BPD symptoms in patients who have both conditions).

It is not a type of Affective Disorder

The symptoms of BPD and affective illnesses are very similar, leading some to speculate that BPD is a variation of an affective disease — either major depressive or bipolar disorder. However, this has not been shown. Although BPD may manifest symptoms that are similar to those of MDD or bipolar illness, experts agree that BPD isn't really a variation of any of these diseases. However, characteristics of both illnesses can manifest themselves in BPD.

The most compelling evidence that bipolar illness is not a variation of major depression is that therapy for melancholy doesn't really result in a remission of symptoms associated with bipolar disorder. Significant longitudinal research discovered that successful treatment of borderline personality disorder (BPD) frequently results in cure of depression and that antidepressants are often only of little value for depressive illnesses that co-occur with a borderline personality disorder.

A review of phenotype, endophenotype, and genotype analogies between BPD and MDD published in 2010 found that BPD differs from MDD in terms of prognosis, heritability, symptomatology, patterns of brain area involvement, neuro-hormonal indices, and sleep design, as well as in terms of heritability. The amygdala hyperactivity, volume alterations in the anterior cingulate cortex, and inadequate serotonin function were all shown to be intertwined in certain biological processes. Specifically, the authors pointed out that in order to get a comprehensive understanding of the similarities and differences between BPD and MDD, both diseases must be examined using the same research design and methodology.

When depressive signs and BPD characteristics were studied together in the context of dysthymic disorder, it was shown that a single component underlying both illnesses best described the likelihood of their co-occurrence, giving a good match with the information. The authors hypothesized that the underlying variables were temperamental, genetic, or early contextual risk factors that were shared by all participants.

Early environmental variables, such as those that promote insecure and disordered patterns of attachment, coupled with a nervous, hypersensitive disposition and subsequent childhood trauma, are known to predispose individuals to BPD, as well as clearly-onset depression as well as disorder. It is possible that some of these health conditions also lead to rapid-cycling bipolar illness in addition to other conditions.

According to family studies, although bipolar disorder and

major depressive disorder are frequent co-occurring illnesses with BPD, impulsivity mental illnesses are more prevalent than affective psychiatric conditions in families with BPD. Research has shown that depressive individuals with bipolar illness do not vary substantially from sad patients without bipolar disorder when it comes to the likelihood of developing bipolar disorder with first relatives. It is important to note that therapy with mood-regulating medications does not result in the complete remission of BPD.

A recent study of the similarities and distinctions between bipolar affective disorder and borderline personality disorder (BPD) came to the conclusion that they are distinct disorders with substantial aspects in common. One of the major distinctions between them was their sense of identity, interpersonal disruptions, family medical history of bipolar illnesses, advantages of medication, and the kind of effective dysregulation they were suffering from.

In a recent study of the connection between bipolar illness and borderline personality disorder (BPD), researchers discovered that the highest overlap occurred in regard to quick bipolar disorder. Both borderline personality disorder and rapid-cycling bipolar illness were characterized by frequent changes in mood, as well as a background of childhood trauma, which included sexual, physical, and emotional abuse, as well as neglect. The presence of dysfunctional ego of the "I am bad" kind, as well as susceptibility to abandonment, were much more prevalent in BPD. The authors of the review dispute whether the rapid-cycling bipolar illness is a type of bipolar disorder or if it is a form of bipolar disorder with simultaneous BPD characteristics.

Inevitably, there remain unresolved concerns regarding the factors that contribute to the things that come of affective illnesses and borderline personality disorder, which can only be addressed via future studies.

Depressive symptoms in BPD in the absence of severe depression Depressive symptoms that arise as part of BPD are often transitory and linked to interpersonal stress. When a connection is reestablished, this kind of "depression" is typically relieved significantly. It is possible that anxiety and depression in BPD could also be used to express emotions (such as rage or irritation) that the individual is unable to convey in more appropriate ways (e.g., helplessness, impotence, disappointment). This kind of "depression" is a maladaptive attempt on the part of the patient to express his or her dissatisfaction with a certain person or circumstance in the patient's life. In such depressing situations, antidepressant medication will not be effective; instead, the patient will benefit from a thorough explication of the underlying emotions, followed by assistance in addressing the issue in more adaptive ways.

According to a cross-sectional evaluation, the transitory depressing symptoms of BPD may be difficult to differentiate from the signs of a severe depressive episode (MDE). In the absence of a comprehensive longitudinal history, this may result in an erroneous diagnosis.

For definitive evaluation of MDE or MDD simultaneously with BPD, a thorough assessment of the depressed symptoms over the last several days and weeks is needed. The clinical definition for MDE in patients are the same as for MDE in the general public: continuously lowered mental state for at least 2 weeks, severe impairment of energy, decreased interest in a regular routine, sleep disruption (which may include fatigue or insomnia), losing weight or gain, enhanced suicidal ideation (which is sometimes preceded by enhanced suicidal or other self-harm), and elevated suicidal or other self-harm. The clinical definition for MDE in individuals are similar; however, despite the fact that the general picture of signs is the same in the general public, the quality of depression in BPD is substantially distinct from that in the typical population.

Conclusion

The management of MDD co-occurring with BPD should be based on a psychological approach that encourages reflection on the patient's own mind as well as the minds of others, such as psychotherapy, meditation, supportive therapy, or mentalization-based treatment. In individuals with borderline personality disorder (BPD), such introspection may, over time, reduce the recurrence of the problematic ways of thinking, interacting, and behaving that contribute to sadness and depressive symptoms. In conjunction with the characteristics shared by successful treatments for borderline personality disorder (BPD) indicated. This approach will assist patients in better understanding themselves and others and may result in long-term improvement, including reduced depression.

When MDE co-occurs with BPD, medication for MDE should be given with careful consideration of the risks of polypharmacy and with the understanding that medicine is not the main therapy for BPD. Leading experts emphasize that treatment for depression overlapping with BPD would not result in a cure of the borderline personality disorder, which needs therapy on its own and must be treated separately.

Chapter 7: Treatment of BPD

Borderline Personality Disorder, also clinically known as BPD, is a personality disorder in which people have trouble controlling their emotions. It implies that individuals with BPD experience strong emotions over long periods, making it difficult for them to readjust to some stable baseline because of an emotionally provoking incident.

It is not only because of your unpredictable emotions and relationships but also because of your uncertain self-identity. Self-image, objectives and even preferences may often shift in a manner that seems perplexing and unclear to the individual. It may lead to impulsivity, low self-esteem, tumultuous relationships, and strong emotional reactions to stresses. Self-harm and other hazardous habits may arise from a lack of self-control.

Many complicated things happen within the BPD brain, as experts are still trying to figure out what it all means. However, if you do have BPD, the brain is always on high alert. Things scare and worry you more than they do other people. The fight-or-flight trigger is readily tripped, and once tripped, it takes over your logical mind, activating primal survival impulses that aren't necessarily suitable for the circumstance.

BPD affects around 1.4 percent of the adult population in the United States. Women account for almost 75% of those diagnosed with BPD. According to a recent study, men may be impacted by BPD but are often misdiagnosed for PTSD or depression.

A BPD diagnosis or characteristic is linked to personal relations, identity, emotions, behavior, and thought issues.

1. Relationships

BPD is linked to tumultuous relationships marked by insecurity, tension, and breakups. Due to black-or-white thinking, relationships with friends and family may be idealized or undervalued. Early in a relationship, there may be a desire to spend much time with a beloved one and disclose a lot of personal information, but this may soon turn into hate. Abandonment fears, whether genuine or imagined, may cause many worries, dread, and wrath. Individuals may engage in frantic attempts to avoid the imagined departure of loved ones by pleading, arguing, or threatening self-harm in a push-pull dynamic.

2. Identity

Individuals with BPD struggle to maintain a consistent sense of their professions, sexuality, values, and kinds of friends. They may experience fast, dramatic changes and thus have no idea who they are or what they want to do with their lives. It may lead to a skewed sense of self and strained relationships.

3. Emotions

BPD is characterized by emotional instability because of excessive sensitivity and difficulties controlling emotions, especially in the face of trivial occurrences. Individuals with BPD may experience rapid mood swings, ranging from joy to sadness to excessive rage in a matter of minutes. Once triggered, it may take a long time to return to a more stable state of mind. Regulating these unexpected emotional surges may be difficult, leaving people with BPD looking empty and powerless. As a diversion or release from mental anguish, punishment against oneself, or representing their inner suffering, individuals with BPD may intentionally hurt themselves or engage in suicidal behavior.

4. Behaviors

Disinhibition is characterized by the propensity to engage in hazardous and reckless behaviors such as spending sprees, binge eating, under eating, reckless driving, stealing, unsafe sex, alcohol and drug abuse, and intentional self-harm as a means of relieving pain in people with BPD. Dissociation is a method of dealing with discomfort that gives the sensation of being "checked out." It may be beneficial at times, but it can also be hazardous while performing tasks when detached.

5. Thinking

Emptiness can be felt physically in the chest or abdomen as if a hole needs to be resolved. Various factors can trigger these feelings, including being let down, anticipating being let down by someone else, an absence of close relationships, or shutting out to avoid emotional outbursts. Individuals with BPD may experience paranoia about threats or threats that do not exist when they are stressed. They may be afraid of being judged by others, so they feel isolated or react aggressively to perceived threats. As a defensive strategy against imagined threats, people who have a history of trauma could be hypersensitive towards their environment.

Because personality and identity are so intertwined, the phrase "personality disorder" may make you feel like something is flawed with who you are. A personality illness, on the other hand, is not a character flaw. In clinical terminology, "personality disorder" refers to a pattern of behavior that differs substantially from the norm. It creates difficulties in various aspects of your life, including your relationships, job, and emotions about yourself and everyone else. But, most significantly, these behaviors may be changed!

7.1: Is BPD curable?

The issue of whether borderline personality disorder (BPD) can be treated is likely to be your first concern if you or somebody you love has been diagnosed with it. Even though there is no cure for BPD, this can be treated. Indeed, the proper therapy may lead to a full recovery and remission.

Many physicians used to think that BPD was incurable and grouped it with other difficult-to-treat illnesses such as antisocial personality disorder (ASPD). Newer therapy methods have helped many people achieve long-term remission from BPD, often without medications, as scientists have learned more about the disease.

Many mental health experts believed that treating borderline personality disorder (BPD) was impossible; therefore, they gave up. BPD, on the other hand, is now known to be curable. BPD has a better long-term prognosis than depression and bipolar illness. It does, however, need a unique method. The basic fact is that most individuals with BPD can often improve, and with the appropriate therapies and support, they can do so quite quickly.

The first step toward healing is breaking dysfunctional thinking, feeling, and acting habits that give you pain. Changing long-standing behaviors is difficult. It will seem strange and unpleasant at first to choose to stop, think, and then behave in new ways. However, you will develop new behaviors that will help you maintain emotional balance and control over time.

Identifying the progress of BPD may have a big effect on how individuals with the condition are treated in the clinic. One of the very first challenges is determining the exact nature of the disease. As previously stated, BPD is often diagnosed in young adults, and doctors should begin looking for signs of the illness at this age. Although the condition seems unstable throughout adolescence, most patients' long-term outcomes are the same as those observed in adults. Patients should be referred to evidence-based psychotherapies as soon as feasible since they are accessible (although the evidence in adolescents is not as strong as it is in adults). There is no justification for delaying care and treatment, and several arguments for delaying diagnosis and treatment (based on the idea that symptoms are transitory) are unfounded. Finally, giving patients a correct diagnosis and information about the usually good outcomes of

BPD may give them hope when they feel hopeless. Evidence indicates that even a short period of diagnosis-related psychoeducation may be helpful.

Some people react better than others; therefore, the results may vary. But, for the most part, BPD may be treated in the same manner that diabetes or other chronic illnesses are managed: with educated and personalized therapy. Although the illness will not go away, it can be treated to improve the quality of life.

According to 2015 research, most persons with BPD may no longer fulfill the diagnostic criteria by the time individuals reach adulthood. As the illness progresses, most individuals seem to outgrow the symptoms and reach remission.

Nonetheless, after therapy for borderline personality disorder, the path to recovery is quite simple. Symptoms of BPD tend to appear in early adulthood and then fade away over time until they are no longer a part of everyday life. The age-related decrease in BPD severity is accelerated when therapy is given, and long-term recovery prospects are high.

70% of individuals who were diagnosed with a borderline personality disorder but also subsequently discharged did not meet the criteria for BPD at some time over the next six years, according to new research. Ninety-four percent of this group had no return of their symptoms but could also stay symptom-free permanently.

BPD has traditionally been thought of being a lifelong illness. Because BPD is so common in acute psychiatric treatment, individuals with the disease are frequently seen by healthcare workers during times of crisis, resulting in the mistaken belief that recovery is impossible. Therefore, this group of sufferers has been severely stigmatized.

However, it's essential to note that these statistics are based on people who have been diagnosed with BPD and have gotten treatment for it. The findings did not reveal what methods of treatment were given or whether maintenance therapies were used. As a result, it's unclear how much different therapies impacted remission rates and if undiagnosed individuals would also outgrow their illness.

While recovery and remission may not always imply a "cure," they indicate that BPD has been successfully treated. As stated in the definition:

1. **Remission:** When you are in remission, you no longer meet the requirements for BPD diagnosis.

2. **Recovery:** Recovery is a term that isn't clearly defined,

but it implies that you can operate in all areas of life for a long time. Holding down a career and sustaining meaningful relationships are examples of this.

For individuals with BPD, symptom-free living is a feasible aim. It isn't the same issue as getting healed. Although borderline personality disorder is incurable, the risk of recurrence is always there, no matter how long someone has been free from its severe symptoms.

However, if BPD patients remain committed to their ongoing therapy programs, take their medications diligently, and as prescribed, monitor their progress, and seek help if they experience any signs of relapse, there is a good chance that recovery will last indefinitely if not permanently.

In summary, people with borderline personality disorder must accept complete responsibility for their health and rehabilitation, and if they do, their worst BPD symptoms may go away. They will not be healed in the traditional sense, but they will reclaim control over the situation and their fates, which is a tremendous accomplishment in and of itself.

7.2: Criteria for Diagnosis of BPD

If you suspect that you or one of your loved one may have a borderline personality disorder (BPD), learning more about the diagnosis may be extremely beneficial. Knowing what to expect may assist you in taking the next crucial step: scheduling an appointment with a medical expert for an evaluation. Borderline personality disorder (BPD) is the most prevalent personality disorder, affecting 2%. It affects 20% of people with a mental health condition.

Personality disorders are a troublesome extension of ordinary personality characteristics; people with mental illnesses are more likely to have unpleasant personality traits and encounter them to a higher extent. Based on their main problems, the diseases are divided into three groups. Cluster A represents schizoid and paranoid disorders, Cluster B represents erratic disorders (antisocial and narcissistic), and Cluster C represents frightened and nervous personality disorders.

The DSM is the authoritative source of medical data for mental illnesses, including BPD and associated diseases, presented by the American Psychiatric Association. The DSM gives various conditions for each condition and defines how several symptoms are required (and how serious the symptoms should be) to justify a diagnosis.

The DSM symptom criteria were established by a group of BPD specialists, including psychologists and psychiatrists. These symptom criteria were developed using the most up-to-date research. However, it's essential to remember that the symptom criteria could be modified when new research emerges. After years of study and discussion, the fifth version of the DSM and DSM-V was published in 2013. In the current edition, the symptoms criteria for BPD are the same as in the previous iteration, DSM-IV.

BPD is a persistent pattern of unpredictability in personal relationships, self-image, as well as mood, as well as significant impulsivity that begins in early adulthood and manifests itself in a range of settings, as shown by five (or more) of the following:

- Feelings of emptiness that last for days, weeks, or months

- Frantic attempts to escape being abandoned, whether real or imagined

- Self-image or feeling of self that is significantly or consistently unstable

- Emotional instability in response to everyday occurrences, such as acute episodic sorrow, irritation, or worry, lasts for a few hours to a few days.

- Spending, sex, drug addiction, reckless driving, and binge eating are examples of impulsive conduct from at least one of the following areas that may be self-destructive.

- Anger that is inappropriate, strong, or difficult to manage, such as frequent outbursts, continuous rage, or repeated physical confrontations

- Splitting is a pattern of insecure and passionate interpersonal interactions marked by extremes in idealization and depreciation.

- Suicidal conduct, gestures, and threats, or self-harming activity regularly

- Paranoid delusions or severe dissociation symptoms caused by stress.

Breaking the dysfunctional thoughts and beliefs, feeling, and acting that is causing you pain is the first step toward healing. It's difficult to break longstanding habits. At first, pausing to think and then acting in new ways may seem strange and unpleasant. But, with time, you'll develop new behaviors that will help you retain emotional balance and control.

A single sign or symptom does not diagnose BPD, and there is no conclusive medical test for it. A health professional ideally diagnoses BPD after a thorough clinical examination that may involve speaking with prior therapists, examining previous medical assessments, and, where necessary, interviews with family and friends.

Finding a mental health expert is the first step if you suspect you have BPD. While doctors specifically educated to handle BPD and address your concerns may be difficult to come by, they exist. Begin by requesting a reference from your primary care physician or ask relatives and friends for suggestions for a local specialist who specializes in your illness.

It may be beneficial to educate yourself about the many successful therapies available, including medication, therapy, and self-help treatments, in addition to working with a therapist. Finally, remember and you're not alone and that individuals with BPD may have normal and happy lives with the right support.

7.3: Effective Treatments for BPD

A good treatment plan should consider your preferences as well as any other co-existing illnesses you may have. Psychotherapy, medicines, and group, peer, and family support are all possibilities for treatment. As a person with BPD learns what works what doesn't, the overall aim of therapy is for them to progressively self-direct their treatment plan.

Although medication may be used, psychotherapy is the most

common treatment for borderline personality disorder. If your health is in danger, your doctor may suggest that you be admitted to the hospital.

Treatment may assist you in developing skills for managing and dealing with your illness. Other mental health problems that often occur alongside borderline personality disorder, including depression or drug abuse, must also be addressed. You may feel much better with yourself and enjoy a more secure, fulfilling life with therapy.

i.   Psychotherapy:

Long-term 'talking therapies are an important part of BPD therapy and are advised as the first line of defense. According to the evidence basis for psychotherapy treatments in BPD, two modifications of cognitive-behavioral therapy are helpful. Psychotherapy aims to assist you in the following areas:

- Concentrate on your present level of functioning.

- Uncomfortable feelings can be managed if you learn to control them.

- Helping you notice your emotions rather than responding to them may help you become less impulsive.

- Improve your connections by being mindful of your

own and others' emotions.

The following types of psychotherapy are effective:

1. **Dialectical Behavioral Therapy (DBT):** DBT is one of the most well-known, well-researched, and commonly used Evidence-Based Treatments for BPD. Linehan developed DBT by implementing dialectics and the strategic thinking of validation into a treatment that concentrates on skills acquisition and behavioral shaping, based on clinical knowledge with homicidal personality disordered patients that did not change with standard cognitive-behavioral therapy intervention. DBT views BPD as the result of a transaction between people born with intense psychological sensitivity and "invalidating environments," or people or systems (e.g., families, colleges, treatment settings, and workplaces) who cannot perceive and understand or quickly respond to their vulnerabilities.

2. **Schema-focused therapy (SFT):** SFT (schema-focused therapy) is an integrated cognitive treatment that alters a patient's personality structure. The therapist utilizes a range of behavioral, cognitive, and experiential methods in twice-weekly individual therapy sessions to concentrate on the therapeutic relationship, everyday living outside of treatment, and previous traumatic events. Unlike other

treatments, which take a more neutral position, SFT promotes a bond between the therapist and the client, a process known as "limited re-parenting." The four schema modes of BPD addressed in therapy are the distant protector, punishing parent, abandoned/abused kid, and angry/impulsive child. Its change method involves altering negative thinking, feeling, and acting patterns and creating healthy alternatives to replace them so that these dysfunctional schemas no longer control the patient's life.

3. **Mentalization-Based Treatment (MBT):** Mentalization is the complicated ability that people acquire to envision the ideas and emotions that are going on in their own and other people's heads to comprehend interpersonal interactions. That is where the mechanism of change is found. BPD symptoms, according to MBT, emerge when a patient ceases mentalizing, resulting in pathological certainty about other people's intentions, a detachment from reality's grounding effect, and a frantic desire for confirmation of emotions via action. Instead of giving comfort and security, attachment relationships become hyperactive, feeding into anxiety and difficulties coping, making the therapy with BPD challenging. MBT attempts to stabilize BPD symptoms by improving the patient's ability to think clearly under the pressure of attachment activation.

4. **Transference-Focused Psychotherapy (TFP):** TFP focuses on the patient's poor interpersonal relations and strong emotional states. In the transference, the patient's intrinsic interpersonal dynamics emerge, and they are collaboratively explored to reconcile the divides between good and evil that create instabilities in emotions and relationships. TFP, like MBT, works by assisting patients in developing more balanced, comprehensive, and coherent modes of learning about themselves and others. TFP consists of two weekly individual treatment sessions that are not supplemented by group therapy. TFP clinicians are urged to seek out supervision. TFP is better suited to therapies delivered by single physicians rather than groups.

5. **Good psychiatric management:** Case management is used in this therapeutic method, which grounds therapy in the expectation of job or school involvement. It aims to make sense of emotionally trying times by considering the interpersonal context of emotions. Medication, groups, family education, and individual treatment may all be used. GPM emphasizes steady occupational functioning above romantic connections and social functioning improvement over particular symptom treatment. The initial stage in psychoeducation to patients and families should be diagnosis disclosure with a description of the disorder's

symptoms, followed by information on the disorder's genesis and good prognosis.

6. **Systems training for emotional predictability and problem-solving (STEPPS):** STEPPS is a 20-week therapy program that includes working in groups with family members, friends, or significant others. In addition to many other kinds of psychotherapy, STEPPS is utilized.

All these treatments effectively treat BPD, but they take a somewhat different approach to the illness. There isn't one that is intrinsically superior to the others. The method you choose is mainly determined by the efficacy of your interaction with a therapist and your willingness to try it.

ii.   Medication:

While medicines are an essential component of any treatment plan, no single substance is specifically intended to treat BPD's core symptoms. Rather, a variety of off-label medicines may be utilized to address a variety of ailments. Mood stabilizers and antidepressants, for example, may assist with mood changes and dysphoria. Low-dose antipsychotic medicine may also help some people manage symptoms like confused thinking.

Although Food and Drug Administration has not authorized any medicines, particularly for the therapy for borderline personality disorder, some medications may assist with symptoms or co-occurring issues, including sadness, impulsivity, aggressiveness, or anxiety. Two kinds of medicines are very suggested. Mood stabilizers have been shown to assist BPD patients with rage and impulse control difficulties, while antipsychotics may help with cognitive and perceptual impairments. If co-occurring illnesses are present, other medicines may be given, such as antidepressants or anti-anxiety medication.

1. **Mood Stabilizers:** Mood stabilizers are psychiatric medications used to treat mood disorders characterized by severe emotional sensitivity such as rapid mood changes. Mood stabilizers, which have long been used to treat bipolar illness, have been proven to decrease symptoms including irritability, aggression, and mood swings.

2. **Antipsychotics:** Antipsychotics may be beneficial in diagnosing BPD, according to a comprehensive review and meta-analysis of 26 randomized controlled trials, particularly for patients with perceptual and cognitive disturbances such as psychosis or dissociative episodes. They may also help with aggression and aggressiveness, as well as emotional instability and impulse control.

3. **Antidepressants:** Although no effect on the fundamental characteristics of BPD has been shown in studies, the

frequent co-occurrence for BPD with major depressive illness suggests that most individuals diagnosed with BPD may benefit from antidepressant therapy.

iii.   Classes on life skills and education:

Techniques and coping strategies that may assist people with BPD in managing their conditions on their own can be beneficial. BPD patients who grasp the intricacies of their disease are more equipped to identify signs early on, enabling them to intervene before things get out of hand.

iv.   Techniques for holistic mind-body healing:

Holistic approaches to health are excellent for reducing stress and increasing self-awareness, which is crucial for BPD patients learning to control their responses to their symptoms. People with BPD lose their capacity to regulate their emotions and self-control, but hobbies including yoga, meditation, Tai Chi, massage, acupuncture, art therapy, music therapy, exercise routines, and wilderness experiences may help them recover their concentration, self-control, and self-confidence.

v.   Co-occurring disorders may need further therapy:

Co-occurring disorders affect most people with BPD at some time in their life. When BPD is identified, any indications of mood disorders, drug use illnesses, mood disorders, and other personality disorders must be treated concurrently in a psychiatric clinic that provides integrated rehab treatments for various illnesses.

BPD patients will get most of their therapy in an outpatient setting. However, inpatient therapy in a residential treatment facility may be required in the early phases of recovery to assist people with BPD get back on track. The intensity underlying borderline personality disorder signs, coupled with the common presence of other severe mental health problems, frequently need more intense therapy at the start of the treatment period, when patients are still far from being healthy and well.

7.4: Thematic Recovery Stages of BPD

The term "recovery" in the context of borderline personality disorder (BPD) might have traditionally been used to describe symptom improvement and the absence of diagnostic criteria. According to longitudinal research, symptom remission is frequent, with recovery rates ranging from 33 to 99 percent. On the other hand, personal recovery takes a more holistic approach and sees healing as a journey rather than a finished product.

Recovery is described in qualitative studies of people with personality disorders as requiring the reconciliation of individual and other representations, which is promoted via interpersonal interactions and community integration. Castillo and colleagues recognized these viewpoints as well, describing recovery as more than just a hierarchical process that begins with healthy cognitive development and progresses to a condition of transitional recovery.

This process included forming hope, objectives, identity, roles, and a feeling of belonging. These phases were comparable to Katsakou and colleagues' objectives, which covered elements related to emotion regulation and other symptoms. These results were validated in a study of people seeking medical treatment for BPD treatment objectives, which revealed that goals included strengthening relationships, creating a sense of self, and increasing one's feeling of wellbeing in addition to symptom reduction.

While these results suggest that the treatment objectives of manualized treatments may be limited, given the parallels between clinical phenomenology and personal recovery domains, there are inherent challenges in comprehending recovery in personality disorders. Individual views may now be more completely integrated into therapy because of recent shifts in personality disorder conceptualization from a categorical to a dimensional approach that focuses on individual characteristics, severity, and functioning.

Individuals seeking specialized care have had their views widely reflected in the literature. While essential, a wider approach that includes people who do not use specialized services, such as those who have difficulties obtaining them or no longer need them, may offer a more representative picture. It is in line with requests to learn more about the experiences of individuals on the opposing extremes of the recovery spectrum. As a result, this research aims to learn more about the experience and perceptions of recovery in people with BPD at various recovery phases. For demonstrating differences, comparisons were conducted between people in the recoverable and not recovered groups.

In BPD, recovery took place in three stages: being stuck, diagnosis, and improved experience. In the last step of the recovery continuum, differences between people mostly in recovered and non-recovered groups were found. Because the transition between phases was erratic, tales were addressed either in the present or past.

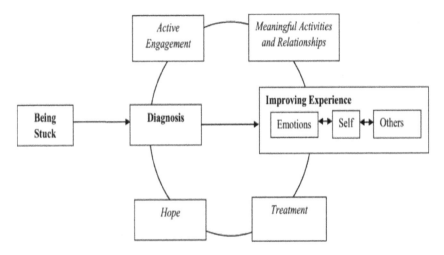

1. Being stuck:

When encountering BPD symptoms for the first time, everyone went through this period. Individuals described being trapped as a condition of floundering in and out of the hospital because they did not have a coherent conceptualization of their experiences. Negative childhood and adolescent events, including bullying or abuse, have impacted individuals' views of themselves and others. During this stage, unsuccessful attempts to seek help for mental issues were also common.

Other psychological health issues, including depression, anxiety, and bipolar disorder, were frequently misdiagnosed.

These diagnoses, according to the participants, did not adequately describe the intensity of their experiences. The ability to acquire effective treatments and the awareness of health professionals were viewed as critical for an individual to keep moving on from the "being stuck" stage.

2. Diagnosis:

Receiving a BPD diagnosis was shown to be a defining moment in helping people understand their experiences and emotional intensity. The effect of delayed or misdiagnosis was emphasized in the amount of time it took to obtain a BPD diagnosis since diagnosis aided some people in receiving evidence-based BPD therapy. A small percentage of people said they didn't accept or care about their diagnosis. While most information was gained via interactions with health care providers, some people recognized their attempts to learn. The stigma and prejudice associated with BPD diagnosis, on the other hand, exacerbated unpleasant experiences.

3. Improving Experience:

A key stage and impact of rehabilitation have increased awareness of emotions, us, and others. This stage was linked to three domains:

- Developing a Greater Consciousness of Emotions and Thoughts

- Self-Esteem

- Becoming aware of other people's viewpoints.

Although these areas weren't mutually exclusive, people progressed at different rates throughout this period. Individuals' perspectives on recovery revealed skepticism about symptom improvement. Survival, resilience, and self-management were all considered important aspects of recovery.

4. Developing a better understanding of thoughts and emotions:

Identifying thoughts and emotions were believed to be a good place to start when developing self-awareness and coping techniques. The recognition of emotions, on the other hand, did not prevent people from becoming distressed.

5. Building one's sense of self:

Everyone agreed that developing one's sense of self was an important part of the healing process. The subtleties of having a better sense of self were described more deeply by those identified as recovered. It was described as a process for redefining one's understanding of or perception of oneself. This process was seen to begin in tandem with the development of abilities in recognizing and tolerating emotions.

Individual narratives addressed a loss of identity resulting from early BPD experiences and how their sense of self was formed because of symptom experience and diagnosis with BPD. A minority of people in the rehabilitated group had difficulty moving away from their disease identity. Despite improvement in recognizing emotions and using skills, there is still a long way to go.

6. Understanding other people's perspectives:

It was a topic that a small number of people in the rehabilitated group addressed, which was characterized by participants as a thinking process beyond one's individual experience to incorporate the potential of others and framework of relationships. An individual's answer emphasized the need to understand others' views in mending relationships. Another person spoke about how the views of others helped her calibrate her self-perceptions.

7.5: Process of Recovery in BPD

This research aimed to obtain a comprehensive knowledge of recovery in people who had lived experience with BPD along either end of the recovery spectrum. Overall, there was a lot of interaction between the phases and processes throughout recovery. Recovery in BPD is described as a continuous process consistent with current research on personal recovery and mental health. Individuals' narratives revealed four recovery stages in BPD:

1. active participation in the process of recovery

2. hope

3. therapy

4. Meaningful activities as well as connections.

These phases may overlap, making the healing process easier or more difficult. Participants in the rehabilitated and non-recovered groups were found to have certain differences. Individuals progressed through the phases of rehabilitation and grew because of these healing processes.

1. Active participation in the process of recovery:

Making progress in recovery required a strong desire as well as a willingness to participate. However, similar observations were frequently made after people had accepted the diagnosis and taken responsibility for learning the skills and doing it themselves.

People in the rehabilitated and not recovered teams had different motivations, with the recovered group emphasizing internal variables and the not recovered team emphasizing extrinsic factors. A small percentage of people said their attitude toward treatment influenced their desire to participate in recovery actively and that a change-oriented mentality was required.

2. Hope:

Hope was an underlying notion that pervaded when personal perspectives or worldviews were favorably contrasted. Recovery was unexpected, and it ushered in a fresh perspective that some people had not considered before. Individuals with feelings of despair, especially in the early phases, were common. Hope may be created via occupational and relational involvement and the following feeling of agency obtained through skill usage or progress review. The capacity to receive therapy was linked to the ability to keep hope for certain people for the not recovered group. Hope led to increases in self-belief and the decrease of self-doubt, which helped maintain the drive. Individuals and their doctors were both affected by the change in viewpoint.

3. Participation in therapeutic services:

Individuals recognized seeking therapy as a critical component of the recovery process, with successful treatment matched with individual objectives providing a feeling of optimism and skill improvement. All the participants reported at least one bad event in which a lack of access to therapy hampered their recovery. When people were at the beginning of the rehabilitation process, they reported having more problems. Inconsistent relationships due to a lack of psychotherapy connection between therapist and patient also contributed to the lack of recovery progress. The progress achieved with therapists who encouraged collaborative and trustworthy partnerships, on the other hand, resulted in stronger connections.

4. **Taking part in activities and relationships that are important to you:**

Meaningful activities and interactions were characterized as giving a feeling of belonging and connection and the chance to practice new abilities, reflect on one's emotional responses, and develop one's sense of self. Although individual variations impacted what was deemed important, job, education, and connections with mates, family, significant others, and physicians were often mentioned. Benefits include independence acquired via employment, as well as a feeling of validation and purpose. Everyone recognized the importance of activities and relationships in terms of self-exploration and reflection. Observing disparities in oneself allowed one to acquire a better understanding of oneself.

The phases of recovery described in this research correspond to

Leamy and colleagues' broad recovery stages. Individuals, on the other hand, framed the phases described clinically. The fundamental psychopathology in BPD was reflected in domains linked with an improved experience. It is like the tasks found in previous qualitative investigations of personality disorder recovery. As a result, the framework created may represent recovery from the perspective of therapy. Individuals in this research experienced an average of ten years of therapy, demonstrating the significance of therapy as part of recovery.

However, research suggests that there are many paths to rehabilitation, including participation in non-traditional psychiatric services. Within the framework of personality disorder, the potential of individual recovery via the use of additional supports, including such social workers or rehabilitation colleges, may be explored further. Despite this, only women's views were considered in the research. Future studies may concentrate on men's views.

The being stuck or diagnosis phases were uniformly reported since participants had to diagnose BPD to participate in the research. The diagnosis provided the chance to construct meaning and encourage hope, which shifted the trajectory of experience. However, there was a 15-year difference between an individual's perception age of onset and diagnosis in this group. It could indicate a knowledge gap among healthcare professionals and the need for clinicians to be up skilled in dealing with clients who have personality disorders or are stigmatized, which could delay diagnosis. This compounds individuals' need for knowledge on BPD at the time of diagnosis.

During the improved experience stage, the differences between both the recovered and non-recovered groups were most noticeable. The recovered team spoke about how they learned about themselves and others, whereas those in the not healed group talked about improving their thoughts and emotions. While development is frequently shown as a step in other wellness concepts, often including self-management of symptoms, the narrative in this research shows that the process of growth started with emotional awareness.

Individuals with BPD are well-known for prioritizing meaningful connections and activities. Interestingly, despite being at opposite ends of the recovery continuum, the percentage of paid work and in a relationship did not vary substantially. It suggests that one's state of recovery may impact the quality of a relationship or the quantity of work one does. In the current research, fewer than half of the recovered people were about or working, suggesting that the current sample could have a more extreme presentation and suffer more psychosocial problems than participants in previous long-term studies. Individuals in the present sample have different treatment contexts than those in longitudinal studies.

It may be related to disparities in the ability to pay for or even obtain treatment. The McLean sample consisted mostly of healthcare insured individuals vs. our group, which was more dependent on overburdened public facilities.

Individuals were recruited from far more than one treatment or service area as part of the study's broad recruitment approach, allowing for a broader variety of perspectives and perspectives to be included. The study, however, used a retrospective approach, which was in line with prior studies. Researchers found it difficult to compare people since healing is not a single entity. People in the not healed group, for example, may have experienced in the past times when they believed themselves to have recovered and may be able to rely on these memories.

Given the large age difference between onset, diagnosis, and present age, individual narratives may be susceptible to some degree of response bias. Future studies may look at using prospectively longitudinal research for map recovery and get real-time reports. The use of a blind data collecting and analysis procedure may help to minimize researcher bias.

Through the experiences of those who have lived through BPD, this research revealed phases and processes related to recovery. The results add to what we already know by comparing people's experiences at opposite extremes of the recovery spectrum. People in the healed group offer a more accurate picture of what the entire recovery spectrum could look like. The results, on the other hand, show that recovery may happen in the setting of therapy. As a result, it's difficult to extrapolate these results to people who seek help for BPD far outside conventional treatment options. A stronger emphasis on individual motivation, therapeutic participation, connections, and hope is suggested in clinical practice to integrate a more comprehensive approach to rehabilitation.

7.6: Co-existing Disorders along with BPD

The presence of two mental disorders in one person is known as BPD co-occurring disorder. These situations are fundamentally distinct for clinical comorbidity, but one disorder can influence the outcome, course, and response to treatment of the other.

It's important to remember that BPD traits or diagnoses are likely to coexist with other psychological disorders like mood disorders, substance abuse problems, and eating disorders. With BPD, the percentage of co-occurring disorders varies by gender. Women are more prone than males to suffer from mood and eating problems. Whereas co-occurring drug use disorders are more common in males.

Bipolar Disorders

Because many of the symptoms of both illnesses appear similar, co-diagnosis of BPD and illness such as bipolar disorder is not uncommon.

The following are common characteristics of BPD as well as bipolar disorders:

- Suicidal ideation or behavior
- Risky sex, reckless driving, or obsessive buying are examples of impulsive, self-destructive conduct.
- Depression and self-hatred are two common symptoms of depression.
- Angry outbursts and irritability
- Personal connections that are shaky
- Abuse of drugs and alcohol
- Feelings of worthlessness or emptiness

Compared to those who just have BP or BPD, those who have comorbid bipolar disorder II with BPD show a compounding impact, especially in terms of emotion regulation deficits, impulsivity, and difficulties with goal-directed behaviors. It is clinically significant since it may indicate a higher risk of self-harm or suicidal behavior.

Therapy for the comorbid bipolar disorders & BPD should follow a multi-tiered approach that includes treating this disorder with a mood stabilizer to improve state-related emotion directive deficits and then engaging in evidence-based psychotherapies to address each emotion regulation shortfall BPD and the bipolar disorder trait domain. To effectively treat stress and regulate symptoms of both diseases, it is essential to strike the appropriate balance.

Eating Disorder

BPD with eating disorders may emerge in youth or early adulthood, and they can coexist. About 54% of individuals with BPD have a past of eating disorders, according to estimates. BPD has been found in about 25% of individuals with anorexia nervosa and 28% of people with bulimia nervosa. These percentages of eating disorders are considerably greater in the BPD group than in the overall population, which is 5-10%. It indicates a significant proportion of individuals with comorbid illnesses who may have long-term functional impairments.

The most common indicators of the emergence of BPD seem to be the inheritance underlying temperament that is sensitive to upbringing and life stresses; the beginning of BPD occurs during the adolescent years. Physical, sexual, and emotional abuse and other forms of childhood trauma are linked to both BPD and eating disorders. According to researchers, BPD develops prior eating disorders, thus knowing and identifying the connection between the two illnesses in a person is critical in determining the optimal treatment path.

Although there is no direct connection between BPD or eating problems, some experts believe there is a causative association. Eating disorders, like BPD, are caused by a combination of biological, psychological, and environmental variables. When combined with a child's susceptibility to discomfort and the media's idealization of slim body types, early exposure to mocking or criticism about appearance may lead to unhealthy dietary behavior. According to certain studies, the neurology of the BPD mind may influence the kind of eating pathology shown in a person. Individuals with BPD may have a variety of eating problems, including:

- self-destructive behavior

- behavior that modifies body shape or food intake

1. IMPULSIVITY AND RISK-TAKING:

Binge overeating, excessive purging, laxative usage, self-induced vomiting, severe restriction to relieve emotional surges, irritation, inappropriate rage, and persistent sensations of emptiness may all be indications of impulsivity as well as risk-taking.

2. Suicidal ideation and self-harm:

Eating disorders are related to sadness, hopelessness, and despair, and they contribute to the greatest mortality rate among all mental health illnesses, with suicide accounting for half of all fatalities. Suicide attempts by individuals suffering from an eating problem are not uncommon.

3. Emotional responsibility:

It may be an effort to find respite from mood instability by participating in impulsive and hazardous behaviors, but eating disordered behavior may also cause mental anguish, hospitalization, family problems, and the medical effect of malnutrition, which can aggravate the stress. It's difficult to say whether strong emotional experiences are caused by emotional or physical stimuli – or a mix of both.

4. States of dissociation:

Malnutrition and dietary deprivation may have serious consequences for one's emotional, psychological, and physical health. Studies on hunger showed that individuals who ate very little food had higher sadness, anxiety, and other emotional and mental consequences.

5. Intimacy difficulties:

People with comorbid anorexia and BPD will hold on to eating disorder habits like a coping mechanism to ease the severe feelings of insecurity or just control over relationships because they believe that being slimmer will make them more attractive or desirable more likely to continue relationships.

Adherence to disordered eating behavior may be seen as either all good or all negative, closely linked to one's self-perception. It results in a volatile sense of self, which may be transferred into interpersonal relationships.

6. Disturbances in identity and a sense of emptiness:

An eating-disordered person may believe that his or her eating problem defines his or her identity. They often claim that the eating disorder acts as their link to the world and their role in it and that without it, they experience profound loneliness and emptiness. Having a severe eating disorder has no benefits since it may consume one's whole identity. Recovery would include finding one's individuality to live a fulfilling life.

Disorders of drug abuse

Researchers discovered that having any mental illness increases the likelihood of lifelong drug dependency in a large

US National Comorbidity Survey Replication. Alcohol, street drugs, and prescription medications are examples of substances. BPD is the second most common personality disorder to have patients who are addicted to drugs or alcohol. About 78 percent of individuals with BPD suffer a drug use problem or addiction at some point in their lives.

Men outweigh women when it comes to comorbid BPD and drug use disorders. People with BPD often misuse alcohol and narcotics to alleviate emotional discomfort momentarily. As a result, the alleviation is fleeting. This co-occurring condition may have a role in BPD men's under diagnosis and treatment adherence.

Substance abuse may exacerbate symptoms of BPD, such as emotional instability, impulsivity, and interpersonal problems, which is a significant problem for those attempting to figure out the link between the two illnesses. Suicidal behavior is also more likely, as are shorter abstinence periods and treatment dropouts. As a result, combining BPD with drug addiction therapy necessitates a unique therapeutic strategy.

Younger individuals have greater rates of coexistence than the overall population when it comes to BPD and drug use disorders. Although age is not a role in either disease, childhood trauma is a frequent characteristic.

According to certain studies, drug abuse problems may lead to BPD and vice versa. Chronic drug usage, for example, may lower serotonin levels, resulting in disinhibition, self-destructive, and impulsive behavior. Individuals with BPD who have neurobiological vulnerabilities may be more vulnerable to the consequences of drug addiction. Substance addiction, for example, may lead to the loss of key relationships and other life stresses, which can lead to BPD in susceptible people.

People with BPD may use psychoactive drugs like opioids, cocaine, or alcohol to self-medicate underlying overwhelming symptoms of emotional distress, developing into drug addiction. Opiates, whether natural or synthetic, relieve pain, and 18.5 percent of individuals with BPD misuse them to alleviate anger or aggressiveness. Cocaine improves mood, confidence, energy, and productivity through elevating mood, decreasing tiredness, and increasing energy and productivity. BPD affects about 16.8% of cocaine addicts. Cocaine users, overall, want to get rid of sensations of emptiness, boredom, depression, or restlessness. Alcohol is abused by 14.3% of people with BPD because it is a depressant that relaxes and sedates stiff emotional discomfort, leaving users dissatisfied.

7.7: Consequences of BPD

In borderline personality disorder, the patient exhibits additional behavioral issues in between violent episodes and frequent displays of rage and repeated physical aggression against others. Suicidal or self-mutilating activities, overspending, indiscreet sexual conduct, drug addiction, theft, and risky driving are common impulsive behaviors.

In addition, there is a significant and persistent identity issue indicated by self-image, sexual orientation, professional aspirations, and other values ambiguity. Manipulation is often used to elicit compassion from others. Violence is often a reaction to rejection by somebody the patient seeks love, care, or just attention. Intense emotional outbursts and emotional instability are often companions to violence.

Although healing of borderline personality disorder seems feasible, therapy should begin as soon as possible once a diagnosis is established since individuals who suffer from the condition may be severely affected by its overpowering symptoms.

- Self-harming behaviors such as piercing, burning, clawing their skin till it bleeds, and so on are common among individuals with BPD.

- Borderline personality disorder will account for 20% of

all psychiatric hospitalizations.

- 78% of people with BPD will acquire an alcohol or drug issue at some time in their life.

- Up to 79 percent of people with BPD will attempt suicide once at least once in a lifetime.

- 10% of people with BPD will commit suicide at some point in their life.

Statistics like these demonstrate the catastrophic impact BPD may have on people if it is not treated in a timely or effective manner.

Patients with BPD spend most of their time in a distant protector mode, attempting to avoid emotions and wants. They isolate themselves from others to avoid being harmed or abandoned. They don't want to speak, feel, or think in this mode, so they use avoidance, keeping people at a distance, using drugs or alcohol, eating disorders, self-injury, dissociation, and sleeping or lying in bed all day achieve this.

Patients frequently feel empty and frigid in this mode, but they prefer it over the emotional turmoil of their family member or friend modes most of the time. Patients with the abandoned-abused past repeat childhood trauma; they feel abandoned, unhappy, hopeless, and powerless. They have intense anxieties about being left alone or being harmed or mistreated. They are very aware of their emotional requirements. However, they are anxious to have these needs satisfied, and even if someone else could care for them, they either cannot accept this person, or this punitive side prevents them from meeting their needs.

Patients with BPD in the furious, impulsive child mode behave rashly to meet their demands and express their emotions in inappropriate ways, such as rage episodes or being too demanding. In the angry kid mode, they may accuse others of not looking for them improperly, putting more pressure on them, for example, by making suicide threats.

Chapter 8: Hardships of BPD

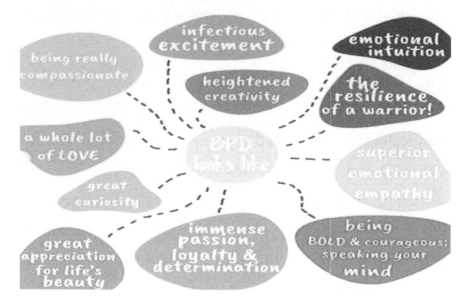

Living to have a borderline personality disorder (BPD) comes with its own set of difficulties. Emotional anguish is frequent, as are emotions of emptiness, despair, rage, hopelessness, and loneliness. These signs and symptoms may have an impact on every aspect of your life. Despite the difficulties, many individuals with BPD manage to deal with their symptoms and live happy lives.

BPD may have a significant effect on your relationships. One of the most common symptoms of BPD is interpersonal problems. People with BPD may have a lot of disagreements and confrontations with their loved ones, as well as a lot of broken relationships. Your daily perception of how you feel towards your relatives, friends, or spouse may vary drastically. Both the individual with BPD as well as those who care for them may struggle with these tendencies.

Work, education, or other useful endeavors may provide us with a feeling of direction in life. Unfortunately, BPD may make it difficult for you to succeed at your job or in education. People with BPD may have problems with coworkers, employers, instructors, or other authority figures since BPD negatively affects relationships. The severe emotional shifts may impact work or school; you may need to be missing more frequently due to emotional issues or hospitalization. Some BPD symptoms, such as dissociation, may interfere with focus, making it difficult to complete activities.

Unfortunately, BPD may have a significant effect on your physical well-being. BPD is linked to several health issues, including chronic pain illnesses like fibromyalgia or chronic fatigue syndrome, glaucoma, obesity, diabetes, or other severe health issues. BPD is also linked to unhealthy lifestyle choices, including smoking, drinking, and not getting enough exercise.

Unfortunately, BPD has the potential to impact your physical health negatively. BPD has been associated with various health problems, including chronic pain conditions such as fibromyalgia and chronic fatigue syndrome, blindness, overweight, diabetes, and other serious health problems. BPD has also been related to poor lifestyle choices such as drinking, smoking, and not exercising enough.

BPD is a severe mental illness. BPD brings with it a slew of difficult experiences that no one should go through alone. There are a lot of effective therapies for BPD, fortunately. One of the essential actions you can take regarding your health is finding a mental health practitioner with whom you feel comfortable discussing symptoms and treatment choices.

8.1: Misdiagnosis

BPD is a complicated disease with symptoms that are comparable to those of many other mental illnesses. Because many mental health practitioners are unfamiliar with BPD and lack training in the field, it's common for BPD to be misdiagnosed as something, such as bipolar illness, because both diseases include mood swings and periods of despair. However, unlike bipolar illness, BPD treatment requires types of therapy instead of a specific drug. The first measure toward feeling better is to obtain a proper diagnosis to get the appropriate treatment.

Why is it so common for BPD to be misdiagnosed?

1. **Symptoms do not emerge immediately after a meeting.**

People with BPD may seem without emotional dysfunctions in surface interactions, such as friends and at first with mental health experts. It isn't because people conceal their BPD symptoms; rather, symptoms emerge as relationships become more intimate and there is a higher level of dependence and dedication towards the other person.

2. **Other mental disorders' comorbidities**. Other mental disorders, such as mental illnesses, eating disorders, and substance use disorder, are more likely to co-occur with BPD traits. As a result, clinicians may miss BPD side effects obscured by symptoms of many other illnesses.

3. **The DSM-IV may be perplexing**. The criteria for BPD in the previous edition of the Diagnostic of Statistical Manual with Disorders (DSM-IV) were extremely unclear, leaving many physicians hesitant to make the diagnosis.

Frequent misdiagnosis of BPD: Bipolar disorders

Bipolar illnesses are a frequent misdiagnosis and comorbid condition with BPD. Both diseases have cross-over characteristics that make it difficult to tell them apart. Both illnesses, however, are thought of differently: BPD is a personality problem, while bipolar disorders are rare brain conditions.

Bipolar illnesses are marked by extreme mood fluctuations that range from euphoric euphoria (mania) to crippling sorrow (depression) (depression). Bipolar disorder follows a similar path from emotional rollercoaster to low; however, the manic (high) stage is less strong and is described as hypomanic.

Specific bouts involving emotional dysregulation in individuals with BPD may mimic hypomania (mood episodes), leading to a misdiagnosis. A person suffering from mania may seem unhappy, impatient, or worried. Both illnesses involve emotional dysregulations, but the dysregulations have distinct sources and expression patterns. BPD is characterized by chronic instead of episodic depression symptoms and a mood heavily influenced by interpersonal events in life. Bipolar illness, on the other hand, produces long periods of depression that may or may not be related to any external circumstances.

Emotion regulation deficits are more severe in people with BPD across a wide range of strategies, such as non-acceptance of feelings and emotions, difficulty accessing coping strategies, misunderstanding and awareness of emotions, problems controlling impulses, catastrophizing, and self-blame. They're also more prone to immediately engage in hazardous behaviors in response to these emotional stresses.

"Situational events influence mood swings in true bipolar patients to some extent, but they are primarily a result of problems of internal mood regulation, which have a biochemical basis and often occur uncontrollably, without any relational trigger," suggests San Diego professor of psychiatry Dr. David Reiss. "On the other hand, borderline mood fluctuations are intimately linked to situational events, especially those that occur inside relationships."

The difference between the two diseases cannot be determined only based on symptoms. As a result, three additional traditional diagnostic validators in psychiatry must be addressed, as indicated in the table below:

	Borderline Personality	Bipolar Illness
Symptoms	Suicidal and self-harming behavior, depersonalization, insecure interpersonal connections, sensitivity to criticism, and detachment are all symptoms of	Symptoms or episodes of manic depression

		depression.
Genetics	Environmental heredity is high.	There is a lot of genetic heritability.
Course	Sexual abuse is quite common.	Sexual abuse isn't very common.
Treatment	Psychotherapies are required, and medicines may be used.	Medication is required, and psychotherapies may be included.
Neurobiology	Non-specific	Degeneration of the hippocampus, amygdala enlargement

Consequences of Misdiagnosis

Bipolar illness necessitates the use of certain medicines that are very successful in treating bipolar disorder patients. Psychotherapies especially developed for BPD are the best evidence-based type of therapy for this disease. Patients with BPD may be denied access to specialized treatment and are more likely to get medicines because of a misdiagnosis, resulting in negative side effects and no sign of remission. For being certain of the diagnosis, patients must be monitored over time. Misdiagnosis may be avoided if you follow these steps:

Doctors and therapists aren't minded readers, so keep that in mind. Being honest and open with a mental health expert about your symptoms is the best way to guarantee an accurate diagnosis. It allows the mental health expert to get a complete picture of your situation and assist you in receiving the best therapy possible.

For individuals with varied BPD characteristics, there are various evidence-based therapies accessible; nevertheless, effective personalized BPD therapy can only be performed after your symptoms or inner thinking processes are disclosed. It is to your best advantage to create a list of your problems and objectives before your diagnostic evaluation.

8.2: Hardships related to employment and education

It is possible to have BPD still and achieve academic and professional success. When BPD symptoms are under control, many people may continue successful jobs. On the other side, some individuals with BPD experience difficulties in their careers, with some being jobless, underemployed, or dissatisfied in their positions.

If you have BPD, you may face a few of the following challenges in your educational and professional life:

- Inappropriate interactions with colleagues, pupils, bosses, and instructors.

- Angry outbursts, depressed moods, maintaining boundaries, and causing conflict are all examples of inappropriate reactions to work/social circumstances.

- Symptoms of BPD, such as dissociation, may make it difficult to focus and stay committed to completing activities.

- All-or-nothing thinking implies you may idealize your school or career until something happens, such as a bad grade or evaluation, which causes you to despise and abandon it.

- Identity issues may make it difficult to commit to a single professional route or degree, causing you to fall behind in your career advancement.

You may also have the following symptoms if your borderline symptoms were contributing to your depression:

- Absenteeism from a job or school/university, as well as tardiness.

- Increased time and concentration are required to develop work/study abilities.

- Staying concentrated on a task is difficult.

- Inability to fulfill job or student responsibilities due to a lack of stamina.

Individuals with BPD are bright, creative, and skilled, even though interpersonal connections may be difficult at times. Having a diagnosis does not inevitably make you a bad candidate for a job or a student. It's all about controlling the symptoms because your talents can show through, just like any other barrier in life.

You may have issues with one or more of the criteria listed above, so keep these in mind while making a job decision. Consider how these symptoms may affect your ability to operate in your chosen profession daily. For example, working in a peaceful and tranquil atmosphere may be preferable if you have stress issues than working in a fast-paced sector.

But don't let BPD dictate your educational and career goals. There are individuals with BPD who have already excelled in a variety of fields. Dr. Marsha Lineham, a therapist, researcher, and founder of Dialectical Behavioral Therapy helping individuals with BPD, is one of the clearest and highly inspirational examples.

Workplace and school-based methods of dealing with BPD symptoms:

- Find someone from outside work to talk to about workplace relationships, including a therapist or a trustworthy friend, to separate work and personal life.

- All-or-nothing thinking is frequent and transitory, so keep track of it so you can stay steady and consistent.

- Make it a workplace objective to build solid and professional connections. At work, pay attention to interpersonal relationships and communication.

When assessing your strengths and shortcomings, remember to consider what you have control over and what you don't, and to remember that you are a person distinct from your diagnosis.

Speak with your therapist about effective symptom management methods and job ideas that are a good fit for your skills and abilities.

8.3: Self-Harm in BPD

Suicide, self-harm, as well as suicide attempts, are all too frequent among people with BPD.

Emotional Distress:

BPD is linked to very distressing negative emotional experiences. Many individuals with BPD say they wish to find a method to get away from these unpleasant events. They may attempt various methods to alleviate their mental anguish, including intentional self-harm, drug abuse, and even suicide.

Duration:

BPD is a long-term illness that may persist for years. Suicidal thoughts are among the most distinctive features of BPD. For months, if not years, people with this disease may contemplate suicide regularly. Despite the reality that there have been successful therapies for BPD, this may lead individuals to believe there is no other way out.

Impulsivity:

BPD is linked to impulsivity, or maybe a desire to act without considering the consequences. In a time of acute emotional distress, people with BPD may participate in suicide conduct without fully understanding the repercussions.

Use of Substances:

BPD is often associated with substance abuse, and substance abuse is a cause of suicide in and of itself. When drug abuse problems are coupled with BPD, it may be a deadly mix. Substance abuse may lead to even more impulsivity, and individuals who abuse drugs can overdose.

Abnormalities in the Brain:

According to brain imaging, individuals with BPD exhibit anomalies in the structure, metabolic, and function of the brain compared to healthy persons. These anomalies seem to play a role in BPD characteristics like impulsivity and aggressiveness linked to suicide conduct.

One research looked at the brain architecture of individuals with BPD who had tried suicide to see whether there was a link between impulsivity, aggressiveness, and suicidal conduct. The individuals were divided into two groups based on the severity of their suicide attempts. There was less grey matter in various brain regions in the "high lethality" group than those in the "moderate lethality" group, indicating that their suicide attempts were highly damaging.

According to comparable research, those with BPD had substantially less grey matter in their brains compared to healthy persons. There was a decreased grey matter in 8 out of nine regions in BPD individuals who had already tried suicide.

There was a decreased grey matter in five regions in individuals with BPD who may not have tried suicide. Compared to the previous research, the greater lethality victims had much less grey matter in certain regions than the low lethality attempters.

8.4: Suicidality in BPD

People who suffer from this condition are more prone to suicidal conduct and commit suicide (BPD). According to studies, approximately 75% of individuals with BPD will try suicide at least once in their lives, and many will attempt several times.

Anyone with BPD may also be more prone than people with any other mental illness to commit suicide. According to estimates, between 3% and 10% of individuals with BPD commit suicide and is more approximately 50 times the incidence of suicide throughout the general population.

A typical pattern of inner behavior defines personality disorders (PDs). These start in adolescent years, are rigid and widespread, contribute to clinically substantial discomfort or impairment, were stable and of long duration, and impact cognition, emotional, interpersonal functioning, and impulse control. Personality disorders are prevalent in practice, with up to 45 percent of all outpatients having personality problems in addition to other diagnoses. Because of the therapeutic difficulties it poses, BPD is perhaps the most studied of these.

BPD is linked to various psychopathologies, including mood swings, impulsive behaviors, and shaky interpersonal connections. BPD patients make an average of three suicide attempts in their lives, most of which are via overdose.

Self-harm (non-suicidal self-injury) is also prevalent in people with BPD. The most common symptom of NSSI is minor wounds to the forearms and wrists. On the other side, NSSI isn't meant to be suicidal; BPD sufferers struggle with emotional control and cut themselves to relieve unpleasant inner states. Cutting reduces emotional stress without implying a desire to die.

While drug overdoses may be life-threatening, the nature and purpose of these actions differ considerably. Patients describe their motive as a desire to flee, and they typically occur after stressful life events. Many instances are motivated by ambiguous motives, including tiny amounts of medicine, and contacting important people for assistance. Even when potentially deadly overdoses happen, patients often call those who can help them.

Suicide attempters and completers are two distinct yet overlapping groups that have been known for a long time. According to a large-scale follow-up study, only around 3% of attempters in an emergency department (ER) perished by suicide. Young women make the most repeated efforts, which diminish with time.

Death by Suicide

Suicide happens in approximately 10% of BPD patients, according to follow-up studies. In prospectively observed cohorts, however, lower percentages (3 percent–6%) have been found. These differences may indicate that patients who consent to be tracked in research trials have less severe suicidality.

Suicides in BPD usually happen later inside the disease process and after a lengthy period of failed therapy. 15-year research showed that the average age at suicide was 30, whereas a 27-year study found 37, with a standard deviation equal to 10. As a result, when patients are young and regular visitors to the ER, they are not at their greatest risk of suicide.

Patients with BPD do, nevertheless, commit suicide. The prevalence of this diagnosis in suicide deaths has been investigated using psychological autopsy techniques, including post-mortem interviews with relatives. PDs were found in approximately half of the patients under age 35 in these investigations, with BPD now the most prevalent kind.

Suicide is "particularly worrisome" among young individuals, according to Pompili's meta-analysis, with a high incidence of suicidal behaviors. However, most Bipolar patients improve with time, and that those who attempt suicide are more likely never to recover.

Males with BPD follow a different pattern than females. A psychological autopsy may identify BPD in almost a third of adolescent suicides, most of whom are male. Males outnumber females in other research of BPD patients that committed suicide. At the point of the deaths, just a few of these individuals were undergoing therapy.

Hospitalization due to Suicidality

Many people with bipolar disorder have numerous unsuccessful suicide attempts throughout their therapy. Numerous psychotherapy trials, multiple medications, frequent hospitalizations, and hospitalization for attempted suicides and threats are linked to these therapies. Despite this, the study literature on treating suicidal thoughts in BPD lacks evidence-based recommendations for preventing suicide death.

Clinicians have long recognized that no algorithms can accurately predict a death result in severe mental illnesses. Despite a vast amount of research in suicide prediction, there is currently no viable method that could be used in practice to predict suicide. At best, doctors are left with commonsense recommendations that aren't backed up by research.

The lack of evidence for prevention, on the other hand, has had little effect on how BPD is managed. When individuals try or threaten suicide, they are often admitted to the hospital. Clinicians understandably wish to be cautious, but the lack of controlled evidence precludes us from establishing that hospital stays are an effective suicide prevention strategy. The American Psychiatric Association's guidelines for the treatment of BPD suggest hospitalization for suicide threats. However, these recommendations, which have never been revised, were based on medical opinion rather than evidence demonstrating that hospital admission had a preventative impact.

Repeated hospitalization for suicide threats and attempts may be counterproductive since it conflicts with outpatient therapy and makes it difficult for patients to work. It may also cause a kind of "regression," with increased symptoms based on the reinforcement of suicidal conduct via behavioral reinforcement. In a crisis, Linehan advises against admitting suicidal patients for more than an overnight stay.

Evidence-Based Treatments

We now know that well-structured ambulatory therapy utilizing techniques specially designed for BPD patients is a successful intervention for most BPD patients. Dialectical behavior therapy (DBT) is the most thoroughly researched treatment, with randomized clinical studies confirming its effectiveness. The primary outcomes include fewer overdoses, fewer emergency department visits for suicidality, fewer self-harm incidents, and fewer hospital hospitalizations. DBT is a kind of cognitive-behavioral therapy that teaches patients how to manage unpleasant emotions in methods apart from cutting or overdosing.

Mentalization-based treatment, transference-focused psychotherapy, schema-focused psychotherapy, and conventional cognitive therapy have all been evaluated in randomized clinical studies.

All these techniques are aimed at the emotional instability (emotion dysregulation) and impulsivity that characterize BPD. Patients with emotional dysregulation and a lack of impulse control are more prone to suicidal behavior, and the prevalence of suicide attempts seems closely linked to these characteristics. As a result, all forms of psychotherapy aim to educate patients on how to step outside of their emotions, self-reflect before acting on things, and better comprehend interpersonal interaction.

In general, well-structured, and specially tailored psychological therapies for BPD patients outperform conventional therapeutic management. This data has been presented in a Cochrane study and a systematic meta-analysis, supporting the hypothesis that certain psychotherapies for BPD are effective. These treatments are usually done in an outpatient setting and do not need hospitalization. BPD patients, according to Zanarini, must "get a life," which means psychiatrists must actively engage them in life objectives such as job and social networks.

On the other hand, pharmacological medications have yet to be shown effective in the treatment of BPD. No clinical studies have shown that effective medication therapy may lead to remission of the condition. A Cochrane study concluded that there was insufficient data to recommend any medicine for BPD patients. Anticonvulsant mood stabilizers have also been found to be ineffective in recent studies. There is also some evidence that antipsychotics may be used for brief periods. Unfortunately, most BPD patients are prescribed several medicines, including antidepressants, mood stabilizers, and neuroleptics, and this trend does not seem to be changing. These procedures do not need hospitalization. Additionally, there is little evidence that pharmaceutical regimens help prevent suicide.

Implications

Chronic suicidal thoughts are one of the most distinguishing features of BPD. Patients suffering from mood disorders may feel suicidal while depressed, but these thoughts typically go away once sad. On the other hand, BPD sufferers may contemplate suicide regularly for months or years before going into remission. Suicidal thoughts will wax and wane with life circumstances, waxing when stressful and fading even when they're not.

Suicide thoughts, on the other hand, are much too frequent to help predict suicidal behavior. However, although individuals who engage in suicidal conduct have a statistically greater chance of dying by suicide, no one can predict who will die by suicide. Suicide deaths are uncommon compared to suicide attempts, which is why algorithms based on risk variables have failed to predict who would die by suicide in large-scale follow-up studies. False positives are the issue those patients that match a profile yet do not commit suicide.

Most individuals with BPD never harm themselves despite experiencing suicidal thoughts for extended periods and numerous suicide attempts. Thus, even though threats are spectacular or blood-curdling, the degree of concern generated for patients with BPD that arrive in clinics and ERs with suicidal thoughts is not always warranted. Clinicians must strive to improve the functionality of these patents and must not be diverted from their treatment duties by suicidality.

Chronic suicidality is exhausting for psychiatrists, yet no one wants to give up a patient in this manner. On the other hand, Suicidality is a part of BPD, and most individuals cannot be managed without taking a calculated risk. Furthermore, promoting ER visits and hospitalization promote the exact behaviors that these services are intended to address.

Hospitalization is not evidence-based, and when suicidal behavior is persistent, admittance to a hospital only offers short respite; most patients persist in having suicidal thoughts following release. While some studies suggest that intense therapy should be provided in a hospital setting, comparable programs may be provided in an outpatient setting. To minimize the risks of repeated hospitalizations, consider day therapy, which has some evidence of effectiveness and provides the benefits of admission (intense care by a skilled professional) without the drawbacks. Day programs, however, typically have long waiting lists and thus are useless in a crisis.

When BPD patients threaten suicide, cut themselves, or overdose, they are frequently held through ERs (or admitted inwards). Fear of lawsuits influences some of these decisions. Clinicians may reduce the likelihood of litigation by maintaining meticulous records, consulting with colleagues regularly, and including families early in therapy.

Based on existing data, it is fair to infer that suicidal individuals with BPD should be treated as outpatients with specialist psychotherapy. Psychopharmacology is still a supplement and a choice. A near-fatal attempt (requiring re-evaluation) or a micro-psychotic episode can both justify hospitalization (requiring pharmacological intervention). We must focus on providing emerging evidence-based treatment approaches designed for this stressful population because we have no concrete proof that death through suicide in BPD could be prevented.

8.5: BPD and Family

Condition affecting members of a family

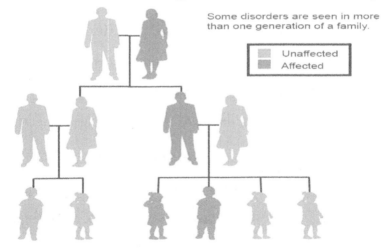

Borderline personality disorder (BPD) seems to be a life-altering mental illness that affects more than just the individual who has it. It influences everyone with whom they have a connection, including friendships, family, and love partners.

Because borderline personality signs and behaviors affect so many family problems, the whole family of a person having borderline personality might suffer. These are among the most frequent family consequences of BPD and where to get assistance as a family.

Stress faced by family members

Seeing a loved one suffer from BPD and coping with BPD's very challenging relationship symptoms may be extremely distressing for family members. When witnessing a beloved one with BPD engaged in self-destructive behaviors, family members frequently feel powerless. It is especially true for family members of teenagers with BPD, who might seem erratic.

Many relatives of the BPD family may suffer significant psychological trauma because of a few of the high-risk behaviors associated with BPD, in addition to the psychological stress of a loved one.

Many individuals with BPD, for example, engage in self-harming activities such as trying to cut or burning. These habits may escalate to the point where they result in death by accident. Furthermore, individuals with BPD have an extremely high suicide rate.

Family members are frequently the ones who must deal with these high-risk activities, such as taking a loved one to the ER after a suicide attempt, and they may suffer psychological trauma, which may develop to issues like post-traumatic stress disorder in extreme instances.

Responsibility and Guilt

Many members of the family of individuals with BPD report their battle with guilt as being very tough. Childhood maltreatment, such as abuse or neglect, may be involved in BPD development, according to focuses on the effects of BPD.

A significant genetic component has also been discovered. Many family members, particularly parents, blame themselves and feel guilty because of these discoveries, even if the growth of their loved one's BPD was beyond their control.

Along with internal conflicts over who is to blame for the establishment of BPD, numerous family members struggle to understand their role in their loved one's rehabilitation.

Some families attempt to be helpful, but they are worried that by doing so, they may be rewarding a few of the BPD-related behaviors, such as self-harm. Others want to be helpful but are irritated by the person with BPD's conduct.

Finally, due to their mental problems, some people find it difficult to be helpful. Because BPD tends to run in the family, other members of the family could also be affected.

Families Face Difficulties

The burden of coping with a loved one's BPD symptoms is made worse by managing their therapy.

Clinicians often turn to the BPD family to organize the family member's therapy, including numerous providers and teams and various levels of care, including outpatient therapy and partial or full hospitalization on occasion.

Family members may be asked to detect changes in their loved one's condition, such as if their mood is lower than normal or whether they take their medicines as recommended, offer transportation to appointments, or coordinate the search for new treatment alternatives. Negotiating these issues and the broader mental health system is no simple job, and it may add to the stress of a family dealing with BPD.

Effects with a Greater Range

Unfortunately, being a person with BPD in the family may cause stress, difficulties, and support problems for both the immediate family.

The tremendous stress that care for a kid with BPD may bring into a marital relationship is described by parents of teens and adults with BPD.

This amount of stress is known to cause marital strife, as well as separation or divorce.

Siblings, too, are impacted in a variety of ways. Some siblings may be drawn into a caregiver role, while others would remove themselves from family to protect themselves, their marriage, children, and other relationships or escape the emotional pain of being in a close connection with someone who has BPD.

Grandparents, aunts, uncles, and other relatives are all part of the BPD family support network, and they may experience the burden of caring for someone with BPD as well.

8.6: Family Experience of BPD

Borderline personality disorder (BPD) patients experience uncontrollable emotions because of interpersonal conflicts. A therapeutic environment where mental health services prevent hospital admissions, self-harm, as well as suicidal behavior help to manage these emotions and achieve a feeling of well-being and control. Clinicians' ability to interact with families could be limited by their knowledge of the disorder's recognized etiology, including a causal relationship to the home environment. Other stumbling blocks include individuals with BPD's negative attitudes toward their families, as well as their doctors' diagnostic doubt or misunderstanding.

The experiences of families with close relatives having BPD have a lengthy past of self-harm and attempted suicides were examined in this qualitative research. Chronic and severe stress was discovered in family members. Family roles and connections, as well as those between the family and the mental health system, we're stressed.

According to the results of this research, therapy for individuals with BPD and their important familial connections needs a comprehensive approach. Relationships between both the family as well as treatment professionals are also important.

Borderline personality disorder (BPD) is a personality condition that affects the individual and others around them. People who suffer from BPD have continuous emotional anguish, typically felt most acutely in their interpersonal interactions. Changes in intimate relationships may elicit powerful and uncontrollable emotions in them. Self-harm and suicidal behavior aid in regulating the self, especially emotions, to regain a feeling of balance, well-being, and control. Second, self-harm attracts others' attention, which is often a desirable outcome.

Because the problems are interpersonal, an interpersonal and relational approach to therapy is required, which involves family work. Multiple barriers to family involvement exist for clinicians contemplating such a strategy.

Suggestions of a causative connection between the family environment and BPD, assumptions, or signs that their client feels negative toward their family, and a condition with a lot of diagnostic ambiguity are among them. Furthermore, family members deal with self-harm or suicidal behavior in a therapeutic setting where hospital stays are avoided and prescribed treatment is delivered in the community.

An increasing corpus of quantitative research examines the relationship between family dynamics and BPD. However, relatively little qualitative research uses family voices to supplement current quantitative studies and provide depth and breadth. In contrast to quantitative research, qualitative research aims to view things from the individuals being researched. A case study accompanying unpublished comments from a focus group discussion indicates many patterns in families' lived experiences with BPD. Some of the topics explored are dealing with numerous diagnoses, living with the person's frequent self-mutilation or suicide threats/attempts, and looking for an understanding of the person's behavior. In addition to problems with the healthcare system and obtaining housing, families faced self-blame, social isolation, and family connection pressure.

The qualitative approach isn't meant to answer questions nor test hypotheses; instead, it's more likely to raise new ones. Any result derived from qualitative research is based on the informants' "views, attitudes, and definitions." My sampling, data collecting, reflection, and analytic methods were all based on grounded theory. Family members could discuss significant issues based on their own experiences and priorities via unstructured, in-depth interviews. After each interview, data were coded for emergent themes to create and propose categories, characteristics, and hypotheses regarding the informants' experiences.

Family members of women who were current or former inhabitants of Spectrum, a specialized statewide Victorian mental health care program, were nominated as informants. The Spectrum resident treatment program has been in existence since 1999, is for individuals with borderline personality disorder prescription, significant interpersonal problems, and lengthy history of self-harm and suicide attempts. Parents were the only ones that were nominated. Both a mother and a father were nominated in two cases, but only the mother consented to be interviewed.

For many years, one mother was separated from her husband. One daughter was still living alongside her parents, while the other two daughters were also single. Both other daughters had kids; one was married, while the other was divorced. An in-depth interview as a technique implies that by asking a specific topic and using an unplanned interview style, one may learn what is most relevant to that source and in that specific researcher and informant setting. The themes that were produced were based on the study data, which reduced researcher inference. Because it is based on the informants' worldviews, this method has a high level of validity. Informants have received a set of interview transcripts and asked to remark on its correctness to help ensure authenticity.

The interviews began with the following questions: "What has been your experience, and your family's experience, with your daughter who has Borderline Personality Disorder? And how do you feel about the various mental health treatment options?" While the informants were not explicitly asked to discuss self-harm or suicidality, they were all aware that the interviewer served for an organization that provided specialized therapy for these issues.

Stress, both Chronic and Traumatic

Parents contacted for this research reported chronic stress because of continuous concern and seeing their daughter hurting herself and coming dangerously close to death.

They used words like 'I can still see it,' 'I can't get the stench out of my nose,' 'This fear is so terrible almost all of the time nowadays,' 'You can't believe how anxious, you know, how exhausted you feel... you don't sleep very much some nights,' and '... a feeling of anxiety when the phone rang,' to describe their experience. The phone would often ring through the night causing eliciting frightened reactions. 'What is this call for?', 'Is it another suicide attempt?', and 'How is she?'; the invasive nature of phone calls helped to reinforce those intrusive thoughts families already had as they struggled to forget about their daughter.

They spoke about their emotional stress, sleep deprivation, and worries about their physical health. Parents were traumatized as well, and one was diagnosed with posttraumatic stress disorder due to seeing her daughter hurt herself and engage in suicidal conduct. Their reactions point to both trauma and posttraumatic stress disorder. Such responses indicate that parents are at high risk of traumatic stress the first time their daughters are severely injured, and as a result, they see such events as startling and out of the usual. Treatment strategies that avoid mental hospitalization or involve only short hospitalizations in response to a crisis were shown to be ineffective and seem to have shifted the responsibility of care to the family. It creates a tension between what might be a helpful treatment approach for the daughter and what is helpful for her family

The Problem of Responsibility and Support

Parents were caught between wanting to continue helping their daughter and dreading the repercussions if they took a step back. Their predicament was exacerbated when medical experts sent confusing or contradictory signals about how much help they should provide. These families battled alone with their problem since health experts did not interact with them in a meaningful way to understand or address their concerns.

Doctors and other mental health experts warned two moms to encourage their daughters' self-harming behaviors by being supportive. Her daughter's doctor had advised her to "support but not over-support." Two mothers were warned that seeing their daughters in the hospital would reinforce their daughters' self-harming and suicidal behavior. One was advised not to look on her kid in the middle of the night to encourage her dependency. As a result, the mother laid awake at night, imagining how she would react if her daughter committed suicide that night. Parents should 'back off and offer less assistance, according to family and friends. One couple expressed concern that their daughter was growing to rely too much on them, but they were afraid of the repercussions of backing off.

Informants also mentioned how essential listening to loved ones, friends, and health experts is, as they provided crucial support throughout these internal battles.

Attempting to Make Understanding of Everything

Parents sadly pondered on their own life and parenting to comprehend their predicament. They studied, spoke to doctors, and researched their genetics, medical, mental wellbeing, and family histories seeking answers.

Two parents discussed how a psychiatrist might help with self-blame. As a result, having a daughter having BPD has caused some parents to examine themselves carefully and seek assistance from other experts in their quest for understanding.

The Effects of BPD on a Larger Family

The mother-daughter connection was occasionally strengthened in the environment of active care, according to the parents questioned. Conflicting emotions of love and rage also marked this passionate connection. As their daughters grew older, two moms believed they would have a close connection with them. When they were diagnosed with BPD, their connection became even stronger. One wanted to assist her daughter, but she was also irritated because she thought she had "given her best at everything but had received so less in return for it." The woman experienced feelings of 'intense compassion' for her daughter at times, and anger against her at others, believing she had 'ripped the family apart.' One mother felt, and the more she, as well as her husband, did, and her daughter acknowledged it, but she insists that "you simply want to do all you can."

Caring for their BPD-affected daughter put a strain on the couple's relationship, particularly when they couldn't agree on how much assistance they should provide. Active-care mothers were divided between caring about the daughter and spending time with their spouse. One woman said that her husband felt she did more for her daughter, while another claimed that the couple's connection was strained, particularly when she was gone often and for many days at a time caring for her daughter.

Other family members, according to informants, had different, and at times harsh, opinions. These differences were a source of conflict and division. Some were worried about the mother's health, with siblings stating, "If you keep going at this pace, you'll die first." Their anxiety also indicates that they accept the potential that their sister's self-harm and suicide behavior may lead to her death.

Siblings seemed less intolerant of their sister's self-harming behavior, according to parents, and were more willing to voice their expectation that she takes responsibility for herself. They influenced their parents' choices on how much assistance they should provide. A sibling advised parents on when to declare "That's not good enough" and which issues to address by stating, "I'm not accepting that."

The parents' marital connection and interactions with her other adult children grew increasingly distant as the mother focused on active care for a BPD daughter. These women would put their daughter first, even if it meant sacrificing their marriage. Siblings have been known to refuse to meet their parents when their sister remained at home, and their emotions have ranged from worry and support to distance and resentment, if not outright hatred.

When siblings had children, family ties were even more strained. The grandparents were unable to devote the time they would have provided to their grandkids. One mother said that her primary concern was to care for her BPD-affected daughter and her children. Her son resented everything his mother did with her daughter's children, as well as the limited time she shared with his own. Parents, siblings, and partners were all afraid that their children would track out their mother and aunt after she had self-harmed.

Mental Health System as well as the Family

Inpatient psychiatric stays were usually short, and one parent believed that hospital stays should be stopped at all costs. The contradiction is that health practitioners gave parent caregivers minimal assistance while relying on them to make treatment choices.

Parents interacted with a variety of services, teams, and individuals. They accessed these services on even a service-by-service basis, oblivious of the interconnections between them and their responsibilities in therapy. As one parent put it, there seemed to be "not a lot of communication" between various teams and doctors at times. Families were confronted with inconsistency and, at times, conflicting counsel, which mirrored one parent's internal struggle.

Individual parents suffered from inner conflict; also, their turmoil was mirrored in the counsel they received from health care providers. While a mother might have the 'nous to listen to others,' the effectiveness of any assistance may be harmed if helpful people express opposing viewpoints.

While informants disliked witnessing a mental health clinician's lack of empathy for their daughter, there had been instances when family members identified the clinician's experience as being like their own. A mother, for example, did not like doctors treating her daughter as just a nuisance, but she could empathize with them since she had had similar feelings.

Following their daughter's admission or release, informants complained about the lack of attention to their needs and concerns. Discharge plans were made without consulting the family. One parent expressed worry that there was no documented treatment plan even when a hospitalization lasted many weeks. Mental health agencies differed in how they communicated with families regarding treatment plans, and therapy seemed to be haphazard at times to parents. Families often saw their interactions with health experts and treatment teams as contrary to the interests of doctors, with nothing more than fact-gathering or information-gathering.

While parents appreciated their daughter's privacy and encouraged her independence, they felt the need for a conversation to give them information, understanding, and comfort in their day-to-day caregiving responsibilities. Meetings might be unpleasant and sometimes frightening, particularly when there were a significant number of doctors present. Parents were unsure of what to anticipate and were hesitant to talk openly or ask specific questions when their daughter was there. Meetings specifically designed with families in mind, with the express aim of working with, supporting, or helping families, were rare.

Chapter 9: Coping with BPD

9.1: Coping Skills Benefits

Your emotions may become overpowering if you do have a borderline personality disorder (BPD). BPD symptoms include mood swings, self-harming activities, suicidality, strong emotional experiences, hypersensitivity to interpersonal difficulties, and impulsive behavior. Emotion dysregulation may be at the root of all these symptoms.

A borderline personality disorder is a condition that makes it difficult for people to deal with a wide range of emotions and ideas. Many individuals with borderline personality disorder are always worried or afraid of being abandoned, whether actual or imagined. People diagnosed with BPD are more prone to self-harm or commit suicide.

You may have extremely powerful emotional reactions and trouble regulating them if you have emotion dysregulation. Unfortunately, many individuals with BPD resort to harmful behaviors like aggression, self-harm, or drug misuse to deal with their emotional anguish. 1 Emotion instability and other BPD symptoms may be reduced with coping skills.

The good news is that a person with a personality disorder may discover new functioning methods and feel better with therapy and support. The bad news is that expert assistance may be difficult to come by in many parts of the globe. Self-help techniques and tactics may frequently help a person cope with their most unpleasant symptoms.

Individuals with this disorder may assist themselves in several ways. Many BPD therapies stress developing coping skills needed to successfully regulate emotions since psychological distress is a prominent characteristic of BPD. What are coping skills, exactly? They are more healthy approaches to dealing with circumstances and the emotions that arise because of them.

Learning new coping mechanisms has the potential to be beneficial. These methods may help you:

- Gain confidence in your abilities to deal with adversity

- Improve the ability to operate effectively even when faced with adversity.

- Lessen the severity of your emotional anguish.

- Decrease the chance of you doing anything dangerous (e.g., self-harming) to escape from emotional pain.

- When you're angry, you're less likely to participate in relationship-destroying behaviors (e.g., physical violence).

- As a result, your overall perspective of emotion dysregulation will be reduced.

People employ hundreds of different coping strategies to deal with stressful circumstances and the emotions that accompany them. Here seem to be a few different kinds of coping techniques that many individuals find useful.

1. Participate in your treatment plan:

Treatment for borderline personality disorder is necessary, and you should strive to be an active, involved participant in whatever program you are enrolled in. You'll feel more confident to ask pertinent questions, offer recommendations, and be honest and open with treatment professionals as you gain more knowledge. There is no one-size-fits-all therapy for

BPD. Getting it right may take some time.

Take some timeout and get to know more about your illness, becoming an advocate for your treatment. You'll feel more powerful as a result, and you'll be more prepared to engage as a collaborator rather than a bystander.

2. Do not be alarmed:

Keep in mind that your prospects of remission are excellent. Early diagnosis and treatment nearly always yield better outcomes than later diagnosis and treatment, like other mental health problems.

3. Seek out experts who have dealt with BPD before:

It not only prevents missed diagnoses as well as comorbidities, and it also increases your chances of getting the most up-to-date therapy with the fewest possible side effects and consequences. Find a therapist who is suitable for you. The foundations of therapy are trust and open communication. Spend the effort to interview a few therapists before settling with one with those whom you feel secure, at ease, and support.

4. Play Music:

Play music that makes you feel the inverse of the feeling you're having trouble with. If you're depressed, for example, listen to cheerful, uplifting music. Play calm, soothing music if you're feeling nervous.

5. Participate in Physical Activity:

The term "behavioral activation" is occasionally used to describe this coping technique. Take part in an activity that is both entertaining and educational. Activities like watching television or using a computer do not qualify since they are too passive. Instead, go on a walk, sing, clean your home, or do anything else that will keep you occupied and divert your attention away from your present feelings.

6. Look for Help:

When you're dealing with intense emotions, reaching out to anyone may be very beneficial. Make a supportive phone call to a family or friend. Contact a hotline if you don't know anybody who can assist you and you're in a crisis.

7. It's a Journey:

Most intense emotional responses and desires to participate in hazardous behaviors peak for another few minutes before fading. Set a 10-minute egg timer in the kitchen. Wait 10 minutes and try to ride off the feeling.

8. Think about it:

Mindfulness of emotions is a good thing to practice. Without attempting to ignore, repress, or hold onto a feeling, notice it, and let it wash over you like a wave. Accept the feeling for what it is, trying to accept it as it is not. Stay in the present as much as possible to avoid bringing your previous feelings with you.

9. Become aware of your surroundings:

Do anything to ground yourself when emotions appear to be pulling you out of the present moment, such as when you begin to feel "zoned out." To break out from negative thoughts, grab an ice cube, hold it in your palm for a few seconds, or snap an elastic band against your wrist.

10. Take a deep breath:

One of the most basic relaxing techniques is deep breathing. Sit or lay down someplace quiet and focus on your breathing. Evenly, slowly, and thoroughly breathe. With each breath, notice how your stomach rises and falls. It may help you remain in the current moment.

If deep breathing isn't enough to calm you down, try a relaxation technique like muscle relaxation.

11. Pray:

Are you a spiritual or religious person? If you attend religious rituals or have contemplated doing so, praying, and visiting weekly congregations may be very beneficial in times of severe stress.

12. Take a Bath or Shower in Warm Water:

Try and lose yourself in warm water's sensations or the soap's aroma. Allow the emotions to take your attention away from the issue bothering you and relax body muscles.

13. Help someone else:

Make a kind gesture for someone else. It wouldn't have to be anything major; you could just go to the closest shop, purchase a pack of gum, and politely say "have a nice day" to the clerk. It may seem little, but simple acts like these may help to alleviate mental distress and link you with the outside world.

14. Grounding Exercises may be beneficial:

You may learn to cope with borderline personality traits by doing grounding techniques. The goal of grounding exercises would be to help you focus your attention on the present moment. The aim is to focus on the now rather than what has happened earlier or what may occur in the future.

Here are some useful examples of grounding exercises:

- **Grounding exercises (visual and aural):** The senses are used in visual and aural exercises to help you return to the present moment. Take a deep breath and glance around while doing visual activities. Consider what you've seen thus far. Try to pay attention to even the tiniest of things. The same thing may be done with an aural grounding exercise – follow the same procedures as a visible grounding exercise but now with sounds instead. Try to pay attention to even the tiniest noises and their peculiarities. The advantage of visual and aural grounding is you'll do it any place, and no one will notice.

- **Exercises in tactile grounding.** Tactile grounding exercises are methods to use your sense of touch to bring oneself into the present moment. There are a variety of methods to put it into practice. Taking a cold shower, for example, maybe beneficial. Wearing an elastic band around the wrist and gently snapping it may assist you in being more present.

- **Using a meditation app to help relax:** Several meditation applications are available to help you center your thoughts and return to a clearer state of mind. To discover the greatest match for you, look through applications on either phone or computer. Using a meditation and relaxation app for a few minutes each day may help you remain focused.

- **Essential oils can be used**. When you're having a

dissociation experience or experiencing symptoms of BPD, aromatherapy using essential oils may help you remain present and peaceful. Look for lavender or chamomile fragrances.

- **Exercising your breathing.** Learn to take slow, deep breaths in via the nose, filling the lungs until they feel like they can't take any more. Then fully expel the air from your lungs via your mouth. Repetition and concentrate on how it feels to expand and then constrict the lungs.

15. Have an emergency preparedness plan in place:

The emotional anguish you feel because of BPD is perhaps one of the hardest challenging aspects of the disorder. It may result in a mental health emergency. You may, for example, experience suicidal thoughts or actions. Establish an emergency safety management system while you are clear-headed in a good mood. Plan for what you'll do if you think you're a danger to yourself or others.

Create a precise strategy since you may not think as effectively while you're in the middle of a potentially dangerous scenario as you did when you made the plan.

16. Obtain Assistance:

If you do have BPD, you may find yourself isolating. You may be feeling alone because you're having trouble with relationships or that you're afraid of being judged. It's essential to have a reliable and trustworthy social support network, such as friends or family.

As a method to build connections, consider attending a community for individuals with BPD.

17. Self-Care is important:

Physical and psychological well-being are inextricably connected. Physical fitness may also assist you in better managing your BPD. A balanced diet, exercise, and enough sleep are all examples of self-care. Find fun methods to relax and relieve stress. You may establish a plan and routine that includes time for your favorite activities.

18. Locate Diagnostic Equipment:

You won't be able to diagnose yourself or perhaps a loved one with borderline personality disorder unless you're a mental health expert. A trained medical expert can only make that diagnosis. However, the technology has provided it simple to take online tests to determine whether you have a borderline personality disorder.

By Googling terms like "depression screening online" or "anxiety test online," you may discover more diagnostic tools. Dr. Kristin Neff's online self-compassion questionnaire is another something I suggest.

Even though these tools aren't ideal, they may help you understand yourself and the symptoms more. Just make sure the test you're taking is trustworthy and was developed using the most up-to-date scientific and medical techniques.

19. Techniques of Mindfulness:

Mindfulness is a technique that encourages people to be more "present" in their lives. It entails being present in the current moment rather than engrossing with past, future, or internal occurrences. It also entails watching events and feelings without being overly judgmental, critical, or analytical.

For the most part, mindfulness is famously tough and requires a lot of effort and careful attention. Other techniques, such as meditation, may aid in achieving this mental state. However, there is good news about mental disorders in general, including borderline personality disorder, since mindfulness may help someone find peace and reduce their symptoms.

Coloring using pencils or markers may be an easy method to cultivate mindfulness for some individuals. Mindfulness is also a key component of dialectical behavior therapy, which has shown potential in treating borderline personality disorder. It may aid in regulating emotions, developing emotional discipline, and the increased focus on feelings and emotions. It may help in reducing signs of depression and anxiety.

Most significantly, mindfulness may aid in the modification of one's brain chemistry, thought patterns, and emotional capability. It may be a useful skill for individuals learning to deal with the symptoms underlying borderline personality disorder.

20. Meditation:

Meditation, like mindfulness, may be very beneficial to someone who has a borderline personality disorder. Indeed, awareness and meditation often go together.

There are many advantages to meditation. Meditation is a technique for calming one's mind that includes slowing down, focusing on ideas, breathing, or chanting. There are many distinct kinds of meditations, each with its own set of benefits.

Meditation has been shown to have many advantages for psychological health in general in numerous research. It may help individuals feel more comfortable and at peace by reducing anxiety and depressive symptoms. It, in turn, may help individuals with borderline personality disorder control their emotional intensity, decrease emotional outbursts, and have better relationships, all of which can significantly affect people with the condition.

Medication or therapy sessions should never be the primary focus of your treatment. You may use a variety of self-help techniques to improve your life. Journaling, creative writing, music therapy, or mindfulness meditation are just a few examples.

According to a research study, individuals with borderline personality disorder who meditate frequently show improvements in various symptoms.

21. Podcasts:

People have been long-time fans of podcasts and know that each episode teaches me something new. Podcasts covering mindfulness, good lifestyles, self-care, and dealing with depression and anxiety may be found. If you're interested, there's a podcast out there for you.

22. Include your family in the process:

A diagnosis of BPD has an impact on the whole family. When people engage in your treatment, it helps to heal emotional fractures that may exacerbate your disease. Not only may family therapy help you recover through BPD, but it could also assist your family.

9.2: Self-Help Guide

Humans have strived to improve themselves and their position in life from the beginning of recorded history. And recognizing one's needs is the first step in utilizing self-help to improve one's life. It may be beneficial to address these requirements both explicitly and generally. It's critical to understand what you'd like to change and what you must do to make it happen.

Since many of our behaviors are entrenched, and some fundamental personality traits may be unchangeable, real change is hard to achieve. However, all habits and personality characteristics may be modified to different degrees. There is still a lot of time to make a change, and with enough work and dedication, you can become the person you would like to be and at least get closer to being that person. Of course, flexibility is beneficial since objectives may change.

According to conventional wisdom, increasing your willpower will help you achieve your objectives. However, achieving those objectives has less to do with continuous willpower and more to do with organizing your surroundings, habits, and circumstances such that you don't have to think about it. If you'd like to break a bad habit, change your surroundings.

Self-improvement may be very beneficial. However, it is critical to use reputable sources. There are a plethora of internet sites and books that are valid, relevant, and useful.

For common issues like stress and anxiety, self-help may be very beneficial. We scan the area for the next disaster on the horizon. It is an issue where self-improvement may be beneficial; it can show you how to overcome worry through basic stress-reduction techniques such as mindfulness and visualization, for example. Another example is stage fright, which is a frequent issue for which self-help may be very beneficial. This kind of worry may quickly escalate into a fight-or-flight situation that is both emotionally and physically exhausting. It may manifest itself as memory lapses, self-doubt, humiliation, and trembling, but self-awareness may help.

It is preferable to engage in self-improvement than to do nothing. It may be just as beneficial as one-on-one care from a trained therapist, depending on the issue at hand. In general, knowledge based on peer-reviewed research is the gold standard to follow; self-help, when done correctly, may be effective.

Three ways to deal with BPD:

i.   Calm the raging emotions

ii.   Learn to manage impulses and cope with stress.

iii. Enhance your interpersonal abilities

Self-help tip 1: Calm the raging emotions

You've undoubtedly spent lots of time battling your instincts and feelings as somebody with BPD, so acceptance may be difficult to comprehend. However, accepting your feelings does not imply that you approve of them or that you are willing to suffer. It simply means that you cease fighting, avoiding, suppressing, or denying your feelings. Allowing oneself to experience these emotions may take back a bunch of their potency.

Try to just feel your emotions without judging or criticizing them. Don't let the fear of being overwhelmed by your future and past drag you down, and concentrate only on the present now. In this case, mindfulness methods may be very beneficial.

- Begin by monitoring your feelings as if you were on the outside looking in.

- Keep an eye on them as they arrive and go; it might help to imagine them as waves.

- Pay attention to the bodily sensations that go along with your emotions.

- Tell yourself you're okay with how you're feeling right now.

- Just because you're experiencing something doesn't imply it's true.

Engage in an activity that engages one or both of your senses:

One of the fastest and simplest methods to self-soothe is to engage your senses. To figure out which sensory-based stimulus works best for you, you'll have to explore. You'll also need various methods for various emotions. What may assist you when you're furious or irritated isn't the same as what might help you when you're numb or sad. Here are a few activities that will help you along the way:

1. **Touch**: If you don't have enough sensation in your hands, try pouring cold and otherwise hot (but not

scorching hot) water over them, holding ice, or gripping an item or the edges of furnishings as firmly as you can. Take a hot shower or bath, snuggle beneath the bed covers, and cuddle with a pet if you're feeling overwhelmed.

2. **Taste:** If you're feeling numb and empty, try sucking some strong-flavored mints and candies, or slowly consuming anything with a strong taste, such as black pepper chips. Try something relaxing, such as hot tea or soup, to help you relax.

3. **Smell:** Light a candle, inhale the flowers, consider aromatherapy, spray your favorite perfume, or make something deliciously smelling in the kitchen. Strong scents like citrus, herbs, and incense may be your favorites.

4. **Sight:** Concentrate on a photograph that catches your eye. It may be anything in your immediate surroundings (a gorgeous flower arrangement, a beloved artwork or snapshot) or something you envision in your mind.

5. **Sound:** When you need a boost, probably listen to blaring music, ringing any bells, or blowing a whistle. Turn on some relaxing music and listen to the sounds of the natural environment, such as wind, birdsong, or the

ocean, to help you relax. If you can't hear the actual thing, a sound machine may help.

Emotional vulnerability is reduced:

When you're tired and stressed, you're more prone to feel unpleasant emotions. As a result, it's critical to look after your physical and emotional health.

Take good care of yourself by doing the following:

- **Eating a balanced, healthy diet**

- **Getting enough quality sleep**

- **Avoiding mood-altering medications**

- **Exercising regularly**

- **Reducing stress**

- **Exercising relaxation skills**

Self-help tip 2: Learn to manage impulses and cope with stress

When you're beginning to feel stressed, use the soothing methods mentioned above to help you relax. But what would you do when negative emotions swamp you? It is where borderline personality disorder (BPD) impulsivity comes into play. You're so eager for relief in the heat of a moment that you'll do anything, even things you realize you shouldn't, like cutting, reckless sex, hazardous driving, or binge drinking. At times you might feel as if your opinion isn't valued enough.

From being in control of your conduct to being in control of your behavior:

It's critical to understand that these spontaneous actions have a purpose. They're coping strategies for overcoming adversity. Even for the shortest time, they make us feel better. However, the long-term consequences are enormous.

Learning to endure discomfort is the first step toward regaining the power of your actions. It's the key to breaking BPD's harmful habits. When you feel the desire to act out, your capacity to endure discomfort will help you put it on hold. Instead of self-destructive actions responding to unpleasant emotions, you will learn to ride things out while staying in charge of the process.

Emotional intelligence mobile apps are a step-by-step, self-guided curriculum that will educate you on how to ride the "wild horse" of overpowering emotions. The applications will show you how to:

- connect with your emotions

- live with a lot of emotion

- deal with frightening or unpleasant emotions

- maintain your composure and concentration, especially in the face of adversity

The toolbox will educate you on how to cope with stress, but that's not all. It will also show you how to transition from just being emotionally shut off to completely experiencing your feelings. It enables you to feel the entire spectrum of good emotions, such as joy, serenity, and satisfaction, often suppressed when you try to avoid bad emotions.

A grounding technique that can assist you in pausing and regaining control:

There aren't many ways to think calmly after the fight-or-flight response has been activated. Rather than concentrating on your ideas, concentrate on how you feel in your body. The grounding technique below is a fast and easy method to stop impulsive, calm down, and recover control. In only a few minutes, this can make a significant difference.

1. **Locate a quiet area** and take a seat in a comfortable posture.

2. **Concentrate on the sensations** you're having in your body. Feel the ground under your feet. Feel the ground under your feet. In your lap, feel your hands.

3. **Take calm, deep breaths** while concentrating on your

breathing. Slowly take a deep breath in. Take a three-count pause. Then gently exhale, stopping for one count of three once more. Carry on like this for a few minutes.

Distract yourself if you're in a dilemma:

Distracting yourself may assist if your efforts to relax aren't working and you're feeling overwhelmed by destructive impulses. All you need would be something to divert your attention from the negative impulse long enough for it to go away. Anything that attracts your attention may help, but the most effective distraction is one that is also calming. Below are a few activities that you can try in complement to the sensory-based techniques described above:

1. **Watch television.** Watch something that might make you feel better, such as a comedy if you're sad or something soothing if you're furious or irritated.

2. **Do something you like that will keep you occupied.** Gardening, painting, playing guitar, crocheting, reading books, trying to play a computer game, or solving a Sudoku or word puzzle are just a few examples.

3. **Put forth a lot of effort**. Cleaning your home, performing yard work, doing groceries, grooming your cat, and doing the laundry are all good ways to divert your attention.

4. **Get moving**. Getting your adrenaline flowing and letting off steam via physical activity is a good method to do both. If you're anxious, consider calming hobbies like yoga or a stroll around your neighborhood.

5. **Make a call to a buddy.** Distracting yourself, feeling better, and gaining perspective may be as simple as talking to somebody you trust.

Self-help tip 3: Enhance your interpersonal abilities

You've undoubtedly battled to establish stable, fulfilling relationships with lovers, coworkers, and friends if you have a borderline personality disorder. It is due to your inability to take a step back and view things from the perspective of others. You tend to misinterpret people's thoughts and emotions, misunderstand how others perceive you, and miss how your actions impact others. It's not that you don't care, but you have a huge problem when it comes to several other people. The first step is to recognize your interpersonal blind spot. Once you stop blaming others, you may begin to work on improving your relationships and social abilities.

Make sure your assumptions are correct:

When you're stressed and negative, as individuals with BPD frequently are, it's easy to misinterpret others' intentions. Check your assumptions if you're aware of this propensity. Keep in mind because you're not some kind of mind reader! Consider other motives instead of rushing to (typically negative) assumptions. Let's suppose your spouse was harsh with you on your phone, and you're now feeling uncomfortable and worried that they've lost interest in you. Before you react to your emotions, consider the following:

1. **Take a moment to examine the many options.** Perhaps your spouse is under a lot of stress at work. Perhaps he's having a particularly difficult day. Perhaps he hasn't yet had his coffee. His actions may be explained in a variety of ways.

2. **Inquire about the person's objectives**. Asking another person what they're thinking or feeling is one of the easiest methods to double-check your assumptions. Check to see whether they meant what they said or did. Try a gentler approach instead of being accusatory: "I may be mistaken, but it seems like..." or "Maybe I'm too emotional, and I get the feeling that..."

Put an end to the projections:

Do you even tend to transfer your bad emotions onto other people? When you're feeling down about yourself, do you strike out at others? Is constructive criticism or feedback seen as a personal attack? If that was what happened, then you might have had a projection issue.

You'll have to learn to press the brakes to combat projection, just as you did to control your impulsive actions. Pay attention to your emotions as well as your bodily feelings. Keep an eye out for stress symptoms, including a racing heart, muscular tightness, sweat, nausea, or light-headedness. When you're in this mood, you're more likely to go all out and say something you'll come to regret later. Take a few calm, deep breaths and pause. Then pose the three following questions to yourself:

1. Do I have a grudge towards myself?

2. Am I embarrassed or afraid?

3. Am I concerned about being left alone?

If the response is affirmative, take a break from the discussion. Tell the other individual that you're emotional and need some time to reflect before continuing the conversation.

Accept accountability for your part:

Finally, it is critical to accept responsibility for your part in your relationships. Consider how your behaviors may be contributing to the issue. What effect do your actions and words have on your loved ones? Do you find yourself viewing the other individual as either all nice or all bad? You will soon realize the positivity in your current relationships when you try and put yourself in those other people's shoes, give people the benefit of the doubt, and decrease your defensiveness.

9.3: Recognize BPD Triggers

Triggers are specific events or circumstances that aggravate or increase symptoms quickly. These may be internally or externally occurrences. BPD triggers vary between people; however, a few are common to all BPD sufferers.

Situations, individuals, or events that aggravate your BPD symptoms are known as BPD triggers. While BPD triggers differ from one individual to the next, a few are extremely prevalent. They may be external (happening in the real world) or internal (just in your mind).

Your past experiences will determine your triggers. For instance, if you were abused as a kid, a news story on child

abuse, a horror movie or even a piece of information in the newspaper may bring those emotions to the surface.

Recognizing Your Triggers

Take a minute to identify the BPD triggers if you haven't already. Unless you're unsure what to say, consider instances in the past years when you had strong emotions, impulsivity, or a desire to hurt yourself. Then reflect on the circumstances that led up to the feeling. Some therapists may advise you to draw up a list of events, along with the feeling they elicited and your response to that emotion.

1. Triggers in interpersonal relationships:

Relationship cues are the most frequent BPD triggers. Many individuals with BPD are very sensitive to abandonment and may react with great anxiety and fury, recklessness, self-harm, or even suicidality when rejected, criticized, or abandoned in a relationship. Rejection of any sort, job loss, and the termination of a relationship are examples of interpersonal life events.

2. Triggers in mind:

Seemingly random thoughts may trigger intense anxiety as well as other BPD symptoms. It is especially true for individuals suffering from BPD because of traumatic experiences like child abuse.

A recollection, place, or picture of a previous traumatic or loss event may elicit strong emotions. Not all flashbacks are painful; some may be of happy moments in the past, reminding us how things are today.

Learn How To Manage BPD Triggers

It's critical to understand what a BPD episode feels like to handle BPD triggers. Although episodes are largely reliant on circumstances and are unique to each person, there are some similar elements.

An episode of BPD is marked by intense outbursts of rage, as well as episodes of sadness and anxiety. In addition, 80 percent of people with BPD have suicidal thoughts and behaviors when during an episode. During an episode of BPD, a person with BPD will go to tremendous lengths to feel anything and becoming more reclusive and avoidant. During these moments, paranoid ideas of everything being out there to get them or hating them are frequent.

Extreme highs, outbursts of pleasure, and pleasant feelings are all examples of episodes. Because people with BPD are impulsive, it's essential to remember that these emotional peaks are also illness incidents. A BPD episode may also manifest itself in risky conduct. Reckless driving, traffic accidents, reckless spending, and even drug addiction are all prevalent.

Nearly 80% of people with BPD have a drug use problem, which exaggerates symptoms and makes episodes more unstable and unpredictable.

Following are some ways to deal with your daily BPD triggers:

1. Recognizing BPD triggers

2. Coping with Triggers

3. Managing Triggers in BPD

1. Recognizing BPD Triggers:

Many individuals diagnosed with BPD face difficulties pinpointing what triggers their symptoms. At times, they may seem to respond "out of the blue," but a deeper examination typically shows the emotional response's precise triggers.

BPD triggers may vary from something as basic as listening to music these days to a more complicated reaction caused by a particular individual.

Here's an activity to help you figure out what your BPD triggers are. You may focus on establishing effective coping skills after understanding how particular people, things, and situations impact your BPD symptoms.

Step 1: Prepare yourself

Prepare yourself with either a pencil or pen, a notebook, a notepad, or whatever method you choose for taking notes. Next, locate a quiet, private space where you may think about and write down your emotions and ideas.

Before and after this activity, make sure you are psychologically prepared and practice excellent self-care. You will also be asked to consider circumstances that cause you to experience unpleasant sensations.

Step 2: Assemble the Columns

Make three columns in your diary on a sheet of paper.

- Write "Trigger" at the top of the first column.

- Write "Emotion" at the start of the second column.

- Write "Response to Emotion" at the start of the third column.

Step 3: Recall an Emotional Experience

Consider the last moment you had a strong unpleasant emotional reaction. Anger, loneliness, fear, sorrow, humiliation, or emptiness are all possibilities.

Make a note of what happened before you experienced the emotional reaction in the "Trigger" box. Keep in mind that a trigger may be either an internal or external occurrence.

Something that occurred in your surroundings, such as a quarrel with a buddy, or something which happened in your head, such as a recollection or idea, may trigger you.

Step 4: Recognize Your Feelings

Fill in the "Emotion" field with your emotional reactions to the trigger. A single trigger may elicit many emotional responses in you.

If you're having trouble identifying your emotions, leave this section blank, but try to identify at least one.

Step 5: Think about what you're going to say

Record your reaction to the feelings you mentioned in the second column in the "Response to Emotion" field.

Perhaps you felt a great deal of guilt in reaction to triggering and self-harmed as a result. Maybe you were furious, but you were able to control your anger by using coping strategies successfully.

Make a note of whatever feeling you were experiencing and your reaction to it. Try not to be too harsh on yourself or cast judgment on how you handled your emotions.

Step 6: Do It Again Using Recent Memories

Identify 2 or 3 recent situations in which you had a strong emotional reaction. Then, for each episode, repeat steps 3, 4, then 5.

Step 7: Keep an eye out for patterns

Examine the list you've made. Look at the "triggers" column. Do you see a trend emerging here? Is there a pattern to the circumstances, people, and things that keep popping up?

Try to pinpoint one or two trigger categories that regularly elicit significant emotions in you. For example, many individuals with BPD say that feelings of rejection are a powerful trigger for their extreme emotional reactions.

Step 8: Maintain Consistency

Add these events to your list in the future when you have strong emotional outbursts. Consider the incident that generated the emotion, your emotional reaction, and what you performed in response to all those emotions for each episode. Check if you can spot any additional trends or triggers while you reflect.

Step 9: Make educated guesses

As you added to your list, you will get more acquainted with the kinds of circumstances that are likely to trigger symptoms.

This understanding will aid you in learning to recognize when a scenario is likely to trigger the BPD.

You'll become able to develop a strategy for dealing with triggers once you can identify and anticipate them.

Step 10: Give Your Opinion

Give your therapist a copy of your list. They may assist you with developing coping skills and methods for dealing with your triggers more successfully.

2. Coping with Triggers:

Your emotions may be overpowering if you do have a

borderline personality disorder (BPD). Unpredictable mood swings, self-harming activities, suicidality, strong emotional experience, sensitivity to issues in your relations, and impulsive behavior problems are all symptoms of BPD. These signs and symptoms may all be linked to one thing: emotion dysregulation.

You may have extremely powerful emotional reactions and trouble regulating them if you have emotion dysregulation. Unfortunately, many individuals with BPD resort to harmful behaviors like violence, self-harm, or drug misuse to deal with emotional pain. Coping skills may assist in decreasing depressive symptoms and other BPD symptoms.

Many ways to cope with your trigger have been explained in detail in the previous parts of this chapter, and you may re-read them for guidance.

3. Managing and Avoiding Triggers:

Avoiding triggers is one technique you may use to control your BPD symptoms. Avoiding triggers may help you feel more stable while you're in treatment and learning crucial coping skills. 3 You'll have more time to practice your abilities in low-risk settings if you keep away from items that trigger your symptoms. You will be unprepared to manage trigger situations if you leap into them before you have a strong foundation from treatment, and you will likely suffer your typical BPD symptoms and outbursts.

How to Stay Away from Triggers:

BPD (Borderline Personality Disorder) is early on in therapy, and it may be beneficial to plan your life to avoid triggers. Some individuals discover that they'll need to remove viewing the news in their daily routine and many other kinds of media. If some people in your life trigger you, you might have to limit your interactions with them as you struggle through the early stages of BPD.

Your therapist may advise you to avoid certain triggers even after you've completed your treatment plan. It's pointless to watch or force yourself through a movie scene that reminds someone of a terrible childhood experience; it will just bring you needless anguish. These are the kinds of minor triggers you may avoid without interrupting your life, from films to sad music.

Other Coping Techniques:

Because avoiding triggers may not always be feasible or desirable, finding alternative strategies to deal with BPD stimuli is essential.

Avoiding triggers is one possibility for your recovery, but it is not a long-term answer for every trigger. While this approach may be very beneficial when engaging with a psychiatrist, you must use it moderation. When the trigger you're avoiding is foreseeable and doesn't significantly restrict your life, avoiding it may be extremely beneficial. On the other hand, avoiding the trigger isn't practical or sustainable if it's unexpected or includes a significant portion of your life.

Conflict in relationships, for example, is a trigger for many individuals with BPD. The only way to fully prevent conflict in relationships is to stop having any because conflict is an unavoidable component of all relationships. Unfortunately, many individuals with BPD find themselves pushing loved ones away for this reason; they may even shun relationships entirely to avoid aggravating their symptoms. This approach is ineffective. It simply serves to exacerbate emotions of rejection and loneliness, resulting in severe symptoms.

Choosing How to Deal with Triggers:

When choosing how to deal with triggers, it's critical to consult with a therapist or doctor. They'll assist you in figuring out whether avoiding them is a good idea. Avoidance isn't a feasible choice for you if preventing a trigger would disrupt daily life in any manner, such as preventing you from going out to work or neglecting your spouse. Instead, your therapist will work with you to create a trigger plan of action or discover another method to deal with the trigger.

Borderline personality disorder symptoms may be triggered or exacerbated by triggers. Learning to recognize those causes is an essential aspect of controlling your symptoms if you have BPD. Avoiding triggers may be beneficial at times, particularly while learning to manage your illness. Other ways of dealing with triggers, on the other hand, become essential as you build and strengthen your connections with people.

9.4: Self-Management in BPD

You may experience like each day is a battle against your conflicting emotions if you have BPD symptoms. Here are some suggestions for dealing with unpleasant emotions daily while also enhancing your long-term comfort and wellbeing.

1. **Suffering from the desire to self-harm:**

Tasks that may help you to manage self-harm:

- Ask for assistance from someone you trust.

- Recognize your self-harm stressors and recognize when the desire to self-harm arises.

- Determine which distractions are most effective:

    1) Apply ice to the area where you wish to

injure yourself.

2) Apply sticky tape to your skin or apply a plaster to your skin and pull it off.

3) Soak in a cold bath.

4) Breathing deeply

- Develop new and healthier coping mechanisms.

- Keep a journal of your feelings and coping mechanisms.

- Maintain a healthy diet, sleep schedule, and exercise routine.

- Make sure people around you are aware of what to do under a crisis.

- Seek the advice of mental health professional.

2. **Sadness, loneliness, and depression are all symptoms of depression:**

Sadness is a tough feeling to cope with, and it has the potential to turn into depression.

What you may do to help yourself:

- Have faith in someone you can rely on.

- Take care of your physical and mental well-being.

- Identify opportunities that you like, and that are soothing to you.

- Make a list of your resiliency skills. Consider the following scenario:

  1) Find your favorite TV program while wrapped under a blanket.

  2) Use a moisturizer with a pleasant scent to massage your hands.

  3) Write down all your bad emotions on a blank piece of paper and tear them up.

  4) Listen to a piece of music that makes you feel good.

- Keep a mood journal

- Seek the advice of mental health professional.

3. Anxiety, tenseness, and panic:

Anxiety develops when people are afraid of anything, such as tension, humiliation, criticism, or rejection. Panic attacks may strike abruptly and unexpectedly during a time of acute anxiety.

Things you may do to help yourself:

- Ask for assistance from someone you can trust.

- Take care of your physical well-being.

- Experiment with relaxing methods

1) Prepare yourself a hot beverage and sip it slowly, taking in the flavor and aroma, as well as the form and weight of the cup in your hand.

2) Exercise your breathing muscles.

3) Make a reality checklist - write down everything that you can think of about what you're doing right now, including the time, date, room color, and so on.

4) Take a hot bath or shower - this may help you alter your mood by providing a relaxing environment and a pleasant physical feeling.

- Take time to recognize your symptoms.

- Keep a journal

- Seek the advice of mental health professional.

4. Dissociation and dispersion:

Everyone uses dissociation as an escape, but it becomes a concern when it conflicts with everyday living or leads to hazardous behaviors. You would probably not see anything happening at first unless someone else alerted you.

Things you can perform to help yourself:

- Take care of your physical well-being.

- Keep a diary

- Create a mental image of a safe location.

- Work on your grounding skills. Consider the following scenario:

1) Chew a clove of garlic or a dash of chili pepper and note the intense aroma and flavor.

2) Clap your hands together and feel the sting.

3) Get a tall glass of chilly water to drink.

4) Go barefoot

- Make a reality check – write or speak the time and date.

- Make sure people around you are aware of doing anything in a crisis.

- Seek the advice of mental health professional.

5. Angry outbursts and long-term dissatisfaction:

Anger can be harmful if uncontrolled or continues for a long time, which may be scary for you and others. As a result, time is crucial for calming down and dissipating rage.

Something you could do to help yourself:

- Recognize potential triggers

- Be aware of your body's warning signals.

- Make time for yourself to think.

- Experiment with "cooling down" methods. Consider the following scenario:

1) Take slow, deep breaths.

2) Tear up the newspaper

3) Smack a pillow

4) Toss ice cubes into the bath and crush them.

5) Use your imagination or visualize a soothing recollection.

- Use cognitive restructuring, problem-solving skills, improved communication, and humor to gain control over your thoughts.

- Work on your anger control abilities.

- Maintain a healthy diet, sleep schedule, and exercise routine.

6. Use of alcohol and other medications:

Drugs and alcohol are used for relaxation, concentration, socialization, boredom, curiosity, escaping issues, and emotional discomfort alleviation. Recreational drugs alter your perception of the world, your emotions, and your behavior.

Overconsumption of substances and the use of illicit drugs pose health, occupational, criminal, relationship, and financial risks.

Accepting that you may possess a problem and seeking assistance is tough. Get the assistance and support they need by being honest with yourself and others.

Things you may do to help yourself:

- Recognize when your drug abuse has gotten out of hand.

- Ask for assistance from someone you can trust.

- Investigate local therapy and support alternatives that are appropriate for you.

- Find healthy coping techniques that work for you.

- Maintain a healthy diet, sleep schedule, and exercise routine.

- Overcome obstacles and keep moving forward

7. Emotional anguish:

Acceptance of your illness may be difficult for people with BPD since they spend so much energy battling emotional dysregulation. Accepting your emotional reactions does not imply that you approve of them or that you are resigned to pain. Stop battling, ignoring, concealing, or rejecting your emotions, and their ability to overpower your logical thinking will be diminished.

Mindfulness methods may help you let go of the possible futures and concentrate only on the present now, without judging or criticizing your emotional responses.

- Step back from your emotions and observe yourself from the outside as a third person.

- Keep an eye on your emotions as they arrive and go.

- Consider the physical reactions that accompany your emotions.

- Tell yourself how you accept the feelings you are experiencing.

8. Communication that works:

It may be difficult to express oneself to people at times. With BPD, reading verbal and nonverbal communications may be very challenging. Remember to accept other people's opinions and to accept that you won't always get it right. Efficient communication is a skill that needs the practice to sustain strong connections, starting with being honest and open to your ideas and emotions.

9. Self-care daily:

It is critical to maintaining your physical and emotional well-being. It will offer you the greatest opportunity of dealing withtough emotions and circumstances while also allowing you to live a happy life.

Conclusion

BPD is a psychological condition that affects how you think and feel of yourself and others, making it impossible to go about one's regular business. Self-esteem problems, trouble regulating emotions and behavior, and history of insecure relationships are all part of it.

You may have a strong feeling of insecurity or instability if you have a borderline personality disorder, and you may find it difficult to tolerate being alone. Even if you desire meaningful and enduring relationships, improper anger, impulsiveness, and frequent mood changes may drive people away.

By early adulthood, most people have developed a borderline personality disorder. The disease seems to be worsening in early adulthood and may improve with age. Don't give up if you do have a borderline personality disorder. Many individuals with this condition improve with therapy over time and may learn to live happy lives.

People with borderline personality disorder could have mood swings and be unsure of themselves and their place in the world. Consequently, their beliefs and interests may shift rapidly.

Borderline personality disorder patients also tend to see things in extreme ends, all good or negative. Their perceptions of others may shift rapidly as well. Someone who is regarded as a friend someday may be regarded as an adversary or betrayal the next. These ebbs and flows of emotions may lead to tumultuous and unstable partnerships.

This book will guide you will all the information you might need along the way, with detailed guidance on BPD diagnosis and treatment and what myths to avoid while getting treated for BPD. Providing previous BPD patients and their family's experience for readers to get detailed guidance on what they might face in the future and how they can overcome it using other people's experience.

Made in the USA
Monee, IL
25 May 2022

97032833R00144